/1250

SCOTLAND'S NORTH SEA GATEWAY

SCOTLAND'S NORTH SEA GATEWAY

ABERDEEN HARBOUR
AD 1136–1986

John R Turner

ABERDEEN UNIVERSITY PRESS

First published 1986
Aberdeen University Press
A member of the Pergamon Group
© Aberdeen Harbour Board 1986

British Library Cataloguing in Publication Data
Turner, J. R.
  Scotland's North Sea Gateway: Aberdeen
  Harbour AD 1136–1986
  1. Harbours—Scotland—Aberdeen
  (Grampian)—History
  I. Title
  387.1′09412′35   HE558.A3/

ISBN 0-08-032463-0
ISBN 0-08-032464-9 Pbk

Printed in Great Britain
The University Press
Aberdeen

DEDICATION

This book is dedicated to those who, over eight and a half centuries, have themselves dedicated their lifes work and labour to making Aberdeen Harbour a safe haven, a great fishing harbour, the largest offshore oil support harbour in Europe, and one of Britain's major sea-ports.

Contents

Illustrations

Preface

The story which unfolds in this book is one of great enterprise in an area of human endeavour seldom recorded. It is a story in which a safe haven has been created for ships sailing the hostile waters of the North Sea. We can but guess at when the story really begins, but recorded history spans eight and a half centuries.

There are many places in the world where the citizens speak with pride about 'Our Harbour'. Sydney in Australia is one such example, competing only with Rio de Janeiro as the world's most beautiful harbour. There the citizens greet every new visitor with the query 'Have you seen our Harbour'? A visit to the harbour, overlooked by its great bridge and unusual opera house invariably follows. The native Aberdonian rarely declaims the beauty of 'Our Harbour', but few visitors to Aberdeen escape the inevitable tour of the harbour which lies surrounded by the City on all sides. Since Aberdeen Harbour plays so important a part in the economy of the City of Aberdeen, of the Grampian Region, and of the North of Scotland and Highlands in general, the enthusiasm and the pride are wholly justified.

The story which follows is written by one who has been very privileged to play a small and modest part in its most recent development. The development of the Harbour however, has been evolved over many centuries, and no doubt the future will hold much further change. There have been many great milestones in the long history of the harbour in the twelfth, fourteenth, sixteenth and eighteenth centuries. This cyclical development is no longer bicentennial, change in the last two centuries has been continuous, and one can but conjecture what the twenty-second, twenty-fourth and twenty-sixth centuries might hold!

Any story narrating a history covering so long a period of time must inevitably contain all too many dull parts and dates—the curse of every schoolboy and schoolgirl. Nevertheless the tale is one of great fascination. It is a tale of great endeavour, of constant skill, and of great professional expertise. It is sadly also a tale of conflict, a tale sometimes of human failing, and from time to time of human duplicity and self-interest. Development of the modern harbour has not all been plain sailing, there have been many bitter moments along the way, and even today there are those who would see affairs handled differently. Inevitably the present busy harbour trade is a source of envy, and of fierce competition from other ports and harbours.

xv

It is hoped that this book will stimulate interest in the Harbour, and will act as a pointer to the real professional historian. No detailed cross-references are given; there is a brief bibliography and, listed in the appendices, a catalogue of relevant Acts of Parliament. The serious history student will have to seek fine detail elsewhere in such well annotated books as the *Shore Work Accounts* of Louise Taylor, and *Port of Aberdeen* by Victoria Clark. Essentially this book paints a broad picture, and tries to steer an acceptable course between a historical fact sheet and a story of human endeavour. If it briefly points the way to the serious history student, and elicits the interest of both native Aberdonians and visitors to North East Scotland, it will have served its purpose.

Much use has been made of the extensive literature covering both Scottish and Aberdeen History. Facts and figures have largely been derived from internal Harbour Board files and statistics, and also from the extensive archives safely preserved in the Harbour Office. Frequent reference has been made to press cuttings over the last century, and to maps spanning the last 300 years or so. Many individuals have come forward with interesting information at different times, and a great debt of gratitude is owed to others who have helped.

I am particularly grateful to my secretary, Miss Beryl Forbes, upon whom has fallen the tiresome task of typing the manuscript and coping with oft-amended drafts. Grateful appreciation is also due to Mr J D Galbraith, Curator of Historical Records, Scottish Record Office, Mr Patrick Cadell of the National Library, Miss Judith Cripps, Archivist City of Aberdeen District Council, Monsignor Charles Burns of the Archivio Segreto at the Vatican in Rome, and the Rt Rev Mario Conti, RC Bishop of Aberdeen. I would also like to thank those who have read the draft manuscript, and have so kindly proferred their advice including Mr J W Cradock, Chairman of Aberdeen Harbour Board, Mr R Mutch of Charles Barker Mearns & Gill, and Dr Grant Simpson of Aberdeen University. I am also particularly grateful to Aberdeen City Libraries, the Aberdeen Maritime Museum, and to Aberdeen Journals for their kind permission to reproduce photographs. The picture of King David I and King Malcolm IV taken from the Great Charter of Kelso Abbey is reproduced by kind permission of the Duke of Roxburghe.

Early Days

One can but guess at the earliest origins of the harbour now lost in the dim mists of time. Few ports anywhere in Britain, or indeed in Europe, can claim such a long history as Aberdeen. It is very hard to be definitive and say exactly when the history of the harbour began since one can only assume and conjecture at the events which preceeded the first recorded reference traditionally ascribed to AD 1136. The first inhabitants of Scotland appear around 5000 BC, and traces of these earlier 'reindeer folk' have been found in many places along the coast. A great quantity of shells and other marine deposits attributed to these pre-historic folk have been found on the 'inches' which were formerly tidal sandbanks or islands in the estuary, where the River Dee flows through what is now the modern harbour, and which now form part of the various quays. Some three thousand years later, new immigrants appeared from Holland and the Rhineland, and evidence of their existence in Aberdeen has been found in the Gilcomston District. These people may well have arrived in the Dee estuary in primitive craft, and almost certainly they used the sheltered estuary as a base for their early fishing expeditions.

Over the succeeding centuries, permanent settlements became established, and were undoubtedly known to the early Roman Legions who initially reached the area under Julius Agricola around AD 84. That Aberdeen was known to the subsequent Roman legions of the Emperor Severus is more certain. Ptolemy's map of Scotland of AD 145 shows *Devana*, a township or settlement on the bank of the *Deva Fluvius*, and this is undoubtedly located somewhere in what has become greater Aberdeen. Some early historians have suggested that the Romans never even reached Aberdeen, but the finding of Roman coins in 1893 suggests that these historians are not correct in their assessment. In all probability, when the Romans built their camp at Normandykes near Peterculter on the outskirts of Aberdeen, their supplies were largely sent in by sea using the sheltered Dee estuary. This would have provided much safer access than the long overland journey, where their supply routes would be subject to constant attack by marauding natives.

1   King David I and King Malcolm IV: from the Great Charter of Kelso Abbey (12th century)

2   Great Seal of David I

The earliest written record of Aberdeen Harbour occurs in a 'Charter' of King David I in which he granted to Bishop Nectan a right to levy a charge on shipping using the harbour. In this Charter, King David transfers the seat of the Bishopric from Mortlach to Aberdeen, and makes arrangements to endow the Bishop with suitable sources of income. The income included a tax or customs duty on shipping trading to Aberdeen.

This particular Charter is reproduced in a book by the Spalding Club entitled *Registrum Episcopatum Aberdonensis*. Cosmo Innes, the editor, believed that this was not the original charter, but a Memorandum recording the Grant to Bishop Nectan which a scribe in a later century had drawn up to resemble an original Charter document, which had disappeared. The method of attesting the Charter was common in the fourteenth century, but was not in use during the time of King David. This testing clause reads:

> *Teste me ipso apud Forfar anno regni mei decimo tertio tricesimo die mensis Junii.* (Forfar, 30 June 1136)

Similarly, the subsequent confirmation of this Charter by King Malcolm IV to Bishop Edward, and dated 8 December 1155, is also regarded by some historians as spurious for the same reasons.

Although it has been suggested that the documents are the work of a later age, there is no doubt whatever as to the authenticity of the original grant. A Bull by Pope Adrian IV clearly and unequivocally authenticates the grants although King David and King Malcolm are not mentioned by name, and this Bull is dated at Sienna on 10 August 1157. The Papal Bull specifically refers to the earlier grants including the dues on shipping, and is to be found in a copy of an inspeximus of the original bull drawn up in a synod at Aberdeen in 1359.

The missing original document might, for want of better explanation, possibly be attributed to the thirteenth century depredations of King Edward I of England. Writing in his *Episcoporum Aberdonensis Vitae*, the Dundee monk, Hector Boece, Principal of Kings College, Aberdeen, suggests that King Alexander II arranged for historic documents and Scottish national records to be transferred from Iona, which was difficult of access, to Restennet near Forfar. Boece, not always accurate in his facts, writing on 31 August 1521, claims that Edward I of England burned these records along with the Priory of Restennet. There is no evidence to support the arguments advanced by Boece, but his argument does seem feasible, and this might account for a fourteenth century scribe producing a replica document. That an original grant existed, however, is not in doubt inasmuch as the Papal Bull, dated only thirty-one years later, quite clearly specifies the grant which is quantified as one-tenth of the cain (on ships). Sadly, no records of Charters, letters or Papal Bulls affecting Scotland in the twelfth century remain in the Archivo Segreto in Rome.

The date of the Charter is recorded as being 30 June in the thirteenth year of the reign of King David. The accession to the throne of Scotland of King David I was 23 April 1124. Some recent historians erroneously attribute the year of the charter to 1134 and others to 1137—the latter presumably by the expedient of adding thirteen to 1124. In fact, however, King David's thirteenth year was from April 1136 to April 1137 so that if the document really was signed in June of the thirteenth year of reign, this must be June 1136. It is a fact that signing must have taken place between 1124 and 1153, and there is no reason to suppose that the scribe who wrote the spurious document would falsify the original date which has ever since been traditionally ascribed to 1136.

Recorded visitations of a decidedly unfriendly nature occurred later in the twelfth century when the Norse Viking King Eystein carried out a vicious attack on *Apardion*—the Norse name for Aberdeen. The Viking recordist waxes lyrical upon this predatory visit:

> I heard the overthrow of people—
> The clash of broken arms was loud,
> The King destroyed the peace
> Of the dwellers in Apardion.

Some years later, the ships of the Viking Leader Swein Asleifsson entered the harbour so that he could join Scotland's king in a round of feasting and merrymaking. The festivities are recorded as having lasted over a month, and probably took place on a site which has been suggested to have been approximately where the present Harbour Office now stands at No. 14 Regent Quay. Although there was no known Royal Palace on the site— certainly this would have been the uppermost limit for navigation by a Viking long ship. This visit by Swein Asleifsson seems to mark the last recorded Viking expedition to the area other than for peaceful trading purposes.

The sheltered estuary of the Dee was undoubtedly the major factor in the development of the town in the thirteenth century. The earliest regular seaborne trade from Aberdeen to the continent was in fact with Flanders. King David I had previously encouraged trade by inviting foreign traders to settle in his Kingdom, and enterprising Flemish merchants had been to the forefront. Privileges were granted to Scottish merchants trading with Flanders, and in 1293 and 1295, King Philip IV of France ordered Count Guy de Dampierre to accord the Scottish merchants freedom of trade with

Flanders. This permitted the Scottish merchants to import wool and other merchandise into France and Flanders, and to live there on payment of the ordinary customs dues. A similar privilege was extended to them by a subsequent charter of Louis de Male in 1395 and later confirmed by Duke Philippe-le-Hardi in 1394, and Duke Jen sans Peur in 1407.

Aberdeen traders subsequently showed themselves anxious to improve trade, and in 1478 paid a part of the expenses of an Embassy to the Duke of Burgundy. At this time, and for many centuries later, control of all commercial matters and of harbour development was vested in the municipal authorities. The first Scottish Consul to the Netherlands was appointed in 1456, and Aberdeen merchants were largely instrumental in effecting this appointment. It is interesting to note the frequent references at this particular period to trade with the Netherlands and Flanders. These close trading links are perpetuated to this day.

Very little was done to create or improve harbour facilities in the middle ages. In 1453, the quayhead had been extended both southwards and eastwards from the Shiprow, and the sum of £50 Scots was expended on renovation work. Thirty years later in 1483, the quay had to be rebuilt suggesting that the initial renovation had not been entirely satisfactory. There was a limited depth of water on the bar, but vessels could remain afloat at anchor in the tidal harbour which was then known by the ancient name of the 'gawpuyl'. The larger vessels were unloaded to smaller craft which would have conveyed the goods to the quayhead along the north bank of the Denburn. The 'peere' or quayhead lay a little to the rear of the line of the present day Trinity Quay. Excavations carried out in 1973 revealed an ancient harbour wall running away from Trinity Quay on a line almost parallel to Shore Brae. A small test trench about thirty feet away confirmed the line of the wall, and all the evidence pointed to this having been the original quayhead. This wall probably dates from the fourteenth or fifteenth centuries, and material dumped in front shows that at a later date there had been constructed a new line of quay. Certainly, this had been done by the time Parson Gordon of Rothiemay drew his map of Aberdeen in 1662.

It was on this original quayhead that the first crane for loading and unloading ships was built in 1582—the idea of one David Endeacht who was given permission to charge 1s. 6d. Scots for each ton carried. It was also in this locality that in the Middle Ages punishments were carried out against wrongdoers. Witches, and those found guilty of adultery, incontinence, swearing, and similar offences, were punished by ducking in the harbour, and some criminals were also drowned off the quayhead in the hollow which came to be known as 'The Pottie'.

At this time piracy was very prevalent in the North Sea. There are many references to the seizure and plunder of Aberdeen ships, principally by the English, but also by many others including the Freisians who had perhaps the worst reputation of all for piracy. The Scots were, themselves, also inclined to indulge in this lucrative business from time to time, and predictably their targets were generally English vessels. The situation became so bad in 1319 that the English King Edward II entreated the merchants of Bruges in Flanders to do no business with Scottish traders, and the Count of Flanders prohibited any contact with pirates, who in the guise of Scots, committed many outrages. In these tough times there seems little to choose between the various perpetrators of piracy on the high seas, and in the absence of any effective naval control, the practice was seemingly very widespread. Apparently the piracy had such a bad effect on the trade of the harbour, that by 1368 the number of ships entering the harbour during the year was reduced to about ten, and thirty years later only six vessels came to the port.

For a time in the fifteenth century, the Hanseatic towns decided to prohibit the importation of Scottish wool, and this naturally had a very detrimental effect on trade. The alliance of France and Scotland, and the subsequent breach with Flanders, resulted in 1424 in the temporary removal of the Scottish staple to Middleburg in Zeeland, and the expulsion of some Flemish traders from Scotland, but by the end of the year the Flemings had sent Ambassadors to Scotland inviting the return of trade to Bruges. Trade was resumed subject to greater privileges being granted to Scottish merchants in Flanders, and from thenceforward trade began to flourish, and the monopoly was divided equally between Aberdeen and Leith. Wool, cloth, hides, furs, and salmon were exported from Scotland, and the vessels returned from Flanders with wheat, provisions, wines, and a variety of luxury consumer goods. The burgh records show that in October 1449 the Aberdeen magistrates, needing funds to repair the parish church, imposed a tithe on every merchant sending goods to Flanders. A further similar levy was unanimously imposed upon themselves subsequently by Aberdeen merchants and exporters in 1518 for the further upkeep of the St Nicholas parish kirk.

Lack of good harbour facilities, however, does not seem to have been any real obstacle because trade from the port continued to develop, and whilst Bruges still remained the centre for Scottish traders, traffic also moved to other ports in Holland and Zeeland as well as to Dantzig and Scandinavia. Bruges was also used as a transhipment and distribution centre for commodities to and from Russia, Scandinavia, England, Scotland, Spain, France, and the Mediterranean. This is paralleled today with the use of the larger continental ports in handling the transhipment goods from many parts of the world where a vessel cannot justify a call at a Scottish port. Ports to which reference is made at this time include Dantzig, Campveere, Bruges, Middleburg, Antwerp, Stralsund, and other Baltic ports. Trade to these latter areas began to develop more extensively in the sixteenth century. At this time many Scots sought better opportunities abroad, and Aberdeen Harbour was the point of emigration for many who sought to avoid poverty, famine, and both the political and religious strife prevalent at home. It is said that Holland was already over-run by Scots at this time, and thus many emigrated to Poland which was then regarded as an attractive field for enterprise. In later years, Robert Gordon of Straloch, with the wealth he accumulated in Dantzig, founded Robert Gordon's Hospital, and many well-known Aberdeen merchants set up cloth manufactures and other forms of business in Poland and Germany. Trade between Aberdeen and the Baltic became so profitable that in AD 1566 a special duty was imposed on all goods imported from Dantzig. Special privileges were allowed to Aberdeen merchants which permitted their vessels to have priority in loading.

About this time problems arose with the health of crews of vessels arriving from overseas ports, and in 1500 a ship entering the harbour from Dantzig, where the plague was raging, had the cargo destroyed by fire, and the sailors were kept in strict quarantine for many days. No food was received from the shore except under the supervision of the magistrate.

This account of the harbour in the earliest times would be incomplete without reference to provision by the city of several vessels for the service of the King. Naval power was virtually unknown in Scotland in the fifteenth century, and ships were fitted out for warfare on an *ad hoc* basis as required by the various sea ports. Around 1475, it appears that three ships of war were supplied by Aberdeen for the King, the funds being raised entirely by the citizens. In 1475 a ship furnished with guns, culverins, ammunition, and other military stores, and manned by twenty-four Aberdeen seamen sailed from the harbour to join the Scottish squadron in the Firth of Forth. The magistrates paid the owners at the same rate of hire as had applied for a similar ship from Dundee. Since Scotland was at peace with England at that time, it is not known for what purpose the fleet was required. Aberdeen Burgh records give an account of steps again taken in 1540 to furnish a warship at the town's expense, and the public funds being insufficient to cover the cost, a general tax was imposed on the burgh. In 1543 a French warship called in Aberdeen carrying letters for the Queen Dowager, the Cardinal, and Lennox. Later, the city joined with other Scottish burghs by

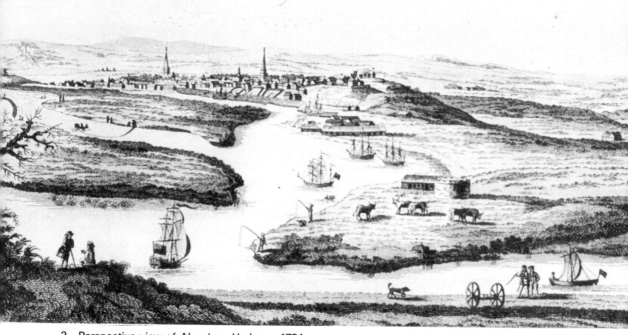

3 Perspective view of Aberdeen Harbour, 1794

contributing toward the fitting out of a ship to carry the Scots Ambassador to France. In 1589, another Aberdeen vessel, meagrely armed, formed part of a squadron sent to bring the King and his new Queen, Anne of Denmark, back to Scotland.

Further efforts began to be made to regulate the operations in the port and to improve facilities. In an effort to reduce the danger to mariners, the Town Council commissioned Robert Lindsay, an Aberdeen Pilot, to furnish the magistrates with a sea chart 'containing many good and profitable instructions for those trading on the sea to foreign lands'. Sadly, neither his chart nor his instructions remain, but for this service he was paid the sum of forty merks—approximately £2 in terms of modern money. In 1511 it was enacted that ships should lie in the 'gawpuyl' and not between the ferry house and the mouth of the river which would have caused obstruction. One such obstruction had been previously caused in 1484 when a Spanish barge lying there, slipped its moorings in a storm and sank, with the result that the channel was blocked for some considerable time. The 1511 regulations imposed a fine for any vessel discharging ballast below the high water mark, and one can imagine the state of congestion which obtained in 1587, when according to a diary of the period, no less than 100 Scottish ships—probably fishing boats for the most part—arrived in the harbour approaches of

Aberdeen and entered the harbour! Around this period of time, firm competition began to arise from other ports, and from time to time Aberdeen protested against the usurpation of its privileges as a free port by Peterhead, Newburgh, and some of the smaller creeks in the locality. It is recorded that in 1573 a number of ships from Norway discharged cargoes at Newburgh, whereupon the Aberdeen City Council issued an order for all ships to unload at Aberdeen and the Dean of Guild and Treasurer was sent to Newburgh to arrest the ships and to remove their sails. The increasing trade had necessitated an increase in duties levied on imports and exports, and this led to numerous attempts to evade port charges. Stringent regulations to enforce the customs were applied, and a ship whose cargo contained goods not entered in the 'cocket' or Clerk's book was declared by the Privy Council (1561) to be unlawfully loaded for the purpose of defrauding the King's custom. At that time any ship found sailing without a 'cocket' was henceforth to be regarded as a pirate and the legitimate prey of anyone. In these circumstances the owners of goods were unable to claim any redress.

The Privy Council Register records an instance where certain Aberdeen merchants allowed their keen business instincts to go beyond the limits of honesty! In 1576, hides constituted a large part of the Aberdeen export trade, and the merchants concerned were charged with packing their skins in such a manner as to defraud the customs. Apparently the skins should have been packed in hundreds of six score, but seemingly 'a greit nowmer ma wass packit'!

In the latter part of the sixteenth century, fears of a Spanish invasion were prevalent, and one rumour was rife that some five to six thousand Spaniards were to land in Aberdeen Harbour to join forces with the Catholic Lords to the North. Certainly Spanish ships used the port at this time to enable Spain to keep in touch with the Earls of Huntly, Errol, and Crawford, but the invasion never came to fruition. A strict watch was kept in 1588 for the Spanish Armada, but their northward flight before Sir Francis Drake and the inclement weather ensured that they passed well clear.

The King of Spain, convinced that the destruction of the Armada in 1588 was due to mismanagement, determined upon another invasion. The second attempt was to have started by the subjugation of Scotland backed by Scottish Catholics, and then invasion of England from the North would have followed. This plan was presumably commended by virtue of the lack of any regular armed Scottish fleet such as the English had under Drake. Aberdeen was at that time the most disaffected area, and on 16 July 1594, the *Esperana* of Calais sailed into Aberdeen Harbour with a party of eminent Catholics who were seized by the Baillies. The group was released after armed men

Aɛt, for a voluntar Contribution tovvards the building and reparing of the Harbour of *Aberdeen*.

Edinburgh, the seventh day of *July*, 1682.

Orasmuch, *as there being a Petition given in to the Lords of His Majesties Privy Council, by the Magistrates, and Town-council of* Aberdeen, *Representing, that the Town of Aberdeen having a considerable Sea trade within themselves, and which is of a considerable advantage to the Countrey, and without a good Harbour, cannot be well managed ; and at the entry thereto, near the mouth of the River of* Dee, *there being by stress of Weather, several Banks casten up, and which is likewise, partly occasioned by the diversion of the Current of the River, which, when running in the middle Channel, did cleanse* the entry of the Harbour from Sand and Banks; *and after serious and deliberate advice, its* found, *that the River cannot well be preserved, in running its due course, without having a* Bulwark upon the North-shore, *as there is one already on the south-side thereof; and whereby the Stream will run in the middle, the building whereof at an equal computation, will cost at least* one thousand pound sterling, *besides the reparing of the Key alongst the Shore, which is of a considerable length ; and which expenses, the Town in regard of the publick burdens, and great debt they ly under, of themselves, are not able to defray it, without that by the Councils Aɛt, they have some assistance of their neighbours, by way of general Collection, as is usual to be granted in the like cases ; and as the Town of* Aberdeen *hath never hitherto been burdensom to their neighbours, in addresses of this nature, so they were never wanting to contribute to the outmost of their power, in the assisting the building of all publick Works, when occasion required ; and as the Harbour of Aberdeen is of necessary use, to preserve the Trade of that place, so the keeping up, and maintaining of the same, is of no less concern to the haill Liedges, and which inevitably will ruine without present supply; And therefore humbly Supplicating, that a voluntar Contribution might be granted, in manner under-written, towards the Building and Reparing of the said Harbour.* The Lords of His Majesties Privy Council, *having heard and considered the foresaid Petition,* Do hereby grant Order and Warrand, *for a voluntar Contribution to be Collected through the haill Kingdom, towards the Building and Reparing of the* said Harbour of Aberdeen; *and Recommend to the Arch-bishops and Bishops, to cause the Ministers in their respective Diocesses, to make intimation of the said Contribution, in their several Paroch Kirks, upon the Lords Day, And ordain* Alexander Anderson, *present Town Thesaurer of Aberdeen, and his successors in the said Office, for the time being, to uplift and Collect the foresaid voluntar Contribution, in regard sufficient Caution is found for them, that what Money shall be Collected, shall be made forthcoming, and imployed to the use foresaid, and to be countable therefore, when required.* Extraɛted by me,

WIL. PATERSON,
Clr. Sti. Con.

GOD save the KING.

under the Earls of Angus and Huntly threatened to burn the town. The second Armada never materialised, but Aberdeen ships were severely harassed by Spanish pirates.

The work begun in 1527 under the direction of the Master of Pierwork, one David Anderson, a master mason, fell into disrepair and substantial repairs were again needed in 1562—it is said that the cost of this was met by the sale of the altar silver of St Nicholas Church which had been sold in a roup for £46. Stormy seas and river floods had, however, continued to take such heavy toll of these harbour works that by 1596 the magistrates once again found themselves desperately in need of substantial funds for harbour maintenance and improvement.

TURNING POINT—THE SEVENTEENTH AND EIGHTEENTH CENTURIES

The seventeenth century represents a watershed in the history of Aberdeen Harbour. As seen in the previous chapter, some earlier work had been carried out to improve the quays, and in fact church silver was used to pay for some of the harbour improvements. By the end of the sixteenth century, however, the position in the harbour had become critical once again, and in 1596 King James VI granted a Charter giving to his Royal Burgh of Aberdeen the privilege of collecting a special levy on all ships and their cargoes entering the harbour. This was for a period of five years, and was to be devoted to the repair of the harbour, and to the construction of a bulwark. These customs and tolls and other duties were subsequently confirmed in further charters over the next few years.

In 1607, a long pier or bulwark was erected on the Torry shore for the purpose of improving the harbour entrance. Detailed records of the payments for construction are still in existence including payments to a piper—an early form of 'music while you work'. The bulwark proved unsatisfactory, and had little effect on the depth of the harbour entrance, and was ultimately removed some 200 years later. In 1610, David Anderson of Finzeaugh, locally known as 'Davie-do-a'thing', removed a large boulder which obstructed the harbour, and in 1623 the quayhead was extended eastward by reclaiming the shorelands between the Denburn Estuary and Fittie Gait. Later, in 1634, the weighhouse was erected on the site of the present Harbour Office near the new quayhead, and three years later a second crane was installed. Two corn mills were built in the harbour area in 1621 and 1631 respectively.

facing page
4   Act of Charles II to raise money for improvements to Aberdeen Harbour, 1682

A record of the sums of money raised from charges on shipping, and the manner in which they were dispersed in order to improve the harbour, are still preserved in the City Archives with relatively few gaps. Details are thus preserved of almost all the traffic to and from the harbour from the end of the sixteenth century until the present time.

The seventeenth and eighteenth centuries must rank as being amongst the most turbulent in the long history of Aberdeen. Alexander Burnett of Leys was instrumental, in May 1639, in petitioning against Montrose who was apparently intent upon blocking Aberdeen Harbour. Seemingly this was to oppose Royalist landing of a force backing the cause of King Charles. Apart from two brief respites, Aberdeen was variously under the harsh regime of Royalist, Covenanter, or Cromwellian. The restoration of the monarchy in 1660 still did not bring prolonged peace to the city, and there was a succession of risings, revolts, and insurrection which all had their effect on the city and limited the trade of the harbour. In 1745, the City welcomed the Duke of Cumberland and his troops, and it was only after the Battle of Culloden that peace prevailed. Inevitably the troubles caused adverse trading conditions thus limiting the traffic of the harbour, and inhibited development of the harbour itself.

5 'New Aberdeine'. A drawing c.1692 showing the 'Gawpuyl' Pocra, and the old Blockhouse which was built in 1477 to defend the harbour entrance.

Despite the civil unrest at home, the commerce of the harbour continued, albeit at a low ebb, to and from much the same ports as in the preceding century. Spain, France, Flanders, and many countries in the Baltic were still closely associated with the East Coast of Scotland. The old privileges enjoyed by trade with France came to an end at the time of the Union of the two parliaments of Scotland and England in 1707, but trading relations with France did continue although often interrupted by warfare. Aberdeen ships plied the old trade routes to Danzig, Königsberg, Stockholm, Gothenburg, Hamburg, Campvere (nowadays landlocked and known as Veere), Rotterdam, Ostend, Havre, Bordeaux, Cadiz, and Marseilles etc. Cargoes comprised salmon, skins, pork, and woollen goods exported, and ships returned with imports of manufactured goods, wines, brandy, sugar, soap, tobacco, and foodstuffs. Additionally there were imports of timber from Germany and the Baltic, together with imports of grain.

New trades were established with Mediterranean ports and elsewhere. It was an Aberdeen shipowner, John Burnet, who pioneered Scottish trade to the New World. Toward the end of the seventeenth century, Aberdeen shipowners joined in a venture to develop trade with Africa and the East Indies, and the Aberdeen magistrates subscribed to the African Company £300 sterling on behalf of the community, but English opposition, and discouragement from the King soon resulted in the dissolution of the company, and financial loss to the shareholders.

The Cromwellian Navigation Act of 1651 was very detrimental to Scottish trade. The effect of the Navigation Act was not the only problem to face traders and shipowners in Scotland, however. There were interminable disputes arising over the shipment of goods to the staple port of Campvere, and goods were diverted for a time to Rotterdam, and Amsterdam to the prejudice of the original trade. Whatever the complaints of the time, however, trade with Aberdeen must still have been inordinately valuable since in 1685, Sir Patrick Drummond, one of the Conservators of Scottish Priviliges in the Netherlands stated that the loss of a single Aberdeen ship was more serious than the loss of 10 ships of other towns.

During the century, a large part of the shipping into and out of Aberdeen Harbour was carried on foreign owned vessels. The size of the ships was very small, and a vessel of 100 tons was apparently a rarity. In 1626, the port apparently possessed only ten vessels averaging about 40 tons, and none of these individually exceeded 60 tons. Many Aberdeen ships were in poor condition, and by the end of the century, in 1692, Aberdeen's entire fleet comprised two vessels of 30 tons each. The larger part of the port's trade was therefore carried in foreign vessels and vessels belonging to other ports.

In Tuckers report of 1656 a clear picture of the condition of the harbour was given as follows:—

The widenesse of the place from the inlett of the sea coming in with a narrowe winding gut and beateing in store of sand with its waves hath rendered it somewhat shallowe in a great part of it and so less usefull of late than formerly. But the inhabitants are remedyeing this inconveniencye by lengthning theyr key and bringing it up close to a neck of land, which jetting out eastward, towards an headland lyeing before it, makes the comeing in soe streight. At the end of which foremost neck of land there is a little village called Footie and at the other headland another called Torye.

Warships, and large vessels were still normally obliged to lie in the river channel or 'Gawpuyll' between Torry and Pocra. Smaller vessels could proceed as far as Footdee, and when tidal conditions were suitable they could proceed on the top of the tide as far as the Town Quay.

Despite the extensive harbour improvements in the early part of the century, conditions appear to have deteriorated so that at low tide there was scarcely two feet of water on the bar. The church, once again, seems to have come to the rescue since an Act of July 1682 provided for a church collection to be taken throughout the whole Kingdom of Scotland toward the building and repairing of Aberdeen Harbour, and Archbishops and Bishops were recommended to persuade the Minsters in each of their respective Dioceses to take up the collection in every parish church. The sums so raised were to be sent to the Town Treasurer of Aberdeen, and then to be utilised for improvement of the harbour. Substantial repairs were consequently carried out to the bulwark, and a new bulwark to the east was constructed.

As a result of the unrest caused by deposition of the Stuart Monarchs, the civil war, the era of the commonwealth, struggles over the national covenant, and other feuds and insurrection, there was no discernible trend in harbour traffic in the seventeenth century, and ship movements fluctuated through out the period. (See Table 1). In 1669–70 the harbour made a deficit of £204.9s. 9d.

In 1669–70 exports from the harbour comprised grain to other Scottish ports, salmon and plaiding and miscellaneous goods to foreign ports, and small mixed cargoes of tar, wine, tobacco, and iron to Scottish ports as well as full cargoes of salt to Scottish ports—presumably transhipped from inward vessels. Imports during 1669–70 comprised grain, salt, wine, wool, timber, onions, iron, coal, slates, lime, and small mixed cargoes.

The Union of the Scottish and English parliaments in 1707 opened up English markets which had hitherto been denied to Aberdeen traders, and

Table 1 Number of Ship Entries and Departures 1596–1670

1596–7	98	1625–6	101	1650–1	112
1597–8	63	1626–7	88	1651–2	90
1598–9	87	1627–8	108	1652–3	121
1599–1600	51	1628–9	128	1653–4	157
1605–6	57	1629–30	95	1654–5	125
1607–8	57	1633–4	102	1655–6	124
1608–9	80	1634–5	125	1656–7	114
1609–10	94	1635–6	99	1657–8	129
1610–11	105	1636–7	104	1658–9	102
1611–12	78	1637–8	75	1659–60	115
1612–13	99	1638–9	68	1660–1	119
1613–14	88	1639–40	64	1661–2	108
1614–15	87	1640–1	116	1662–3	109
1617–18	96	1641–2	101	1663–4	88
1618–19	112	1642–3	111	1664–5	87
1620–21	116	1643–4	96	1665–6	128
1621–2	143	1644–5	88	1666–7	106
1622–3	138	1645–6	98	1667–8	146
1623–4	130	1648–9	95	1668–9	121
1624–5	104	1649–50	84	1669–70	135

this gave an impetus to the trade of the harbour along with development of new markets in North America, West Indies, Madeira, and the Mediterranean. The Statistical Account of Scotland 1791–92 Lists exports from Aberdeen. (See Table 2).

Trade to and from London increased, but the old traffic with Campvere in Zealand continued—if on a reduced scale. The centuries-old tradition of trade between Aberdeen Harbour and Campvere resulted in a recommendation in 1738 that a vacancy at the Scots Kirk in Campvere be filled by an Aberdonian, and ten years later, in 1748 the freedom of Aberdeen was conferred on the Burgomaster of Campvere John Ludovic Ver-Elst.

Trade with the American colonies gained in importance. Many Aberdonians emigrated to the new world and the West Indies, and tobacco and sugar were imported in large quantities. Exports comprised woollen and linen goods, salmon, salted herring, transhipped wines from France. Toward the end of the century, more exotic imports appeared including mahogany, walnut, cotton, coffee, rum, pimento, ginger, indigo, cedar, rosin, turpentine, etc. The eighteenth century also saw the start of whaling.

Clearly, the increasing level of activity in the harbour demanded better facilities. Peter May's map of 1756 shows a new pier having been built in

Table 2

PORT OF ABERDEEN—An Account of the Quantity and Species of Merchandise exported from this Port in the year 1712, shewing the particular Countries to which exported, the number of Vessels employed, their Tonnage, and Number of Men.

To what Country Exported	No of Vessels Employed	No of Tons	No of Men	Species and Quantities of Goods

Norway	13	406	64	1087 3/4ths quarters oatmeal
				1051 ditto barley
				4 ditto pease
				951 3/8ths quarters malt
				146 hundred 1 qr and 500 cod
				    and ling fish at 6 score to the
				    hundred
				7 trusses worsted stockings

Holland	6	238	38	479 barrels salmon 17 hogheads tobacco 359 one-half barrels pork 104 trusses woolen cloth & worsted stockings 10 casks hog lard
Portugal	2	85	14	398 bars lead 10 chaldrons coals 12 trusses worsted stockings 380 cod and ling fish 373 barrels salmon
Sweden	2	100	13	18,690 cod and ling fish 115 3/8ths quarters oatmeal 197 3/8ths quarters malt 90 barrels herrings
Spain	2	150	17	69 one-half barrels salmon 14,052 cod and ling fish 31 parcels worsted stockings 76 barrels herring
Germany	1	40	4	79 3/8ths quarters oatmeal 100 quarters malt 95 5/8ths ditto barley 766 one-half barrels salmon 2 boxes stockings
Italy	4	300	53	90,000 stock fish 47,160 cod and ling fish 68 barrels herring 480 bars lead
Total	30	1319	203	

1743 in the Torry Pool, and a new pier built in 1755 at Pocra. In 1708 the Weigh House had been improved and refloored with timber salvaged from a shipwreck, and some of the timber was also used to construct the head of the south pier. In 1726 the shipmasters had petitioned the Town Council to provide poles on the north side of Torry Pool—presumably for mooring posts, or channel markers—and it is likely that around this period, the posts on the north side of the inches opposite Footdee were installed.

About this time, there appears to have been some recognition of the importance of regular maintenance of harbour structures. Hitherto piers and bulwarks had been initially constructed, but no further maintenance occurred until a state of collapse was reached, and repairs were then so extensive that the overall cost far exceeded the costs of regular maintenance. In order to provide regular inspections and repair of harbour structures, Arthur Gibbon of Torry, was appointed Overseer at a salary of £18 Scots.

Gibbon's duty was to inspect all piers three times per week, and all damage was to be repaired instantly. During weeks when he worked on repairs, he

6 Former Weigh House built in 1634 and demolished in 1897. The present Harbour Office stands on this site.

and staff engaged by him, were paid a regular wage. Gibbon was answerable directly to the Master of Shore Works, and any failure to report necessary repairs was punishable by a deduction of £3 from his annual retainer. The appointment of an overseer had been long overdue, and it would appear that along with the collector, this was still the only full time professional harbour staff in the eighteenth century.

There were repeated complaints about the stairs leading to the shore, and repairs were put in hand. The magistrates also agreed to a proposal to build an office at the head of the shore near the custom house, and this office was in use until replaced by the present Harbour Office building in 1884.

In 1742 the Fish Market was removed from Castle Street to the head of the old shore at the foot of Market Street, and in 1751 a Harbour Overseer, forerunner of latter day Harbour Masters, was appointed to supervise the dumping of ballast. It had been the habit to dump ballast on piers from which it was washed in stormy weather. The Harbour Overseer also had responsibility for regulating ships moorings. It seems that the first incumbents were not altogether effective because the pier built at Pocra in 1755 had to be rebuilt in 1763 because of damage sustained by the old quay as a result of mooring malpractice.

The great turning point in harbour construction occurred in 1769 when the Town Council invited the great eighteenth century engineer, John Smeaton, to investigate the harbour entrance, and to suggest remedial measures to create greater depth at the bar. Smeaton, whose report of 1770 is reproduced in full in an appendix, recommended the construction of a pier at the north side of the harbour entrance on the Sandness. To defray costs, extra charges had to be imposed, and the Act of 1773 received Royal Assent on 1 April. On the recommendation of Smeaton, John Gwyn was appointed engineer to supervise construction at a salary of £120 annually for five years. Arthur Gibbon, the overseer, was instructed to build a lighter to carry the stones and other materials used in the construction.

Some historians have unfairly accused Smeaton of poor design, arguing that the pier was built too far to the north, and that his design should have forseen the inrun of heavy easterly swells. On the first count, time has proved Smeaton correct, and in fact the modern harbour may have benefited had the pier been built even further to the northward. On the second count criticism is not altogether fair. The success of Smeaton's pier in greatly improving the depth of water on the bar certainly did allow the inrun of heavy swells from

facing page
7   Aberdeen Harbour 1746

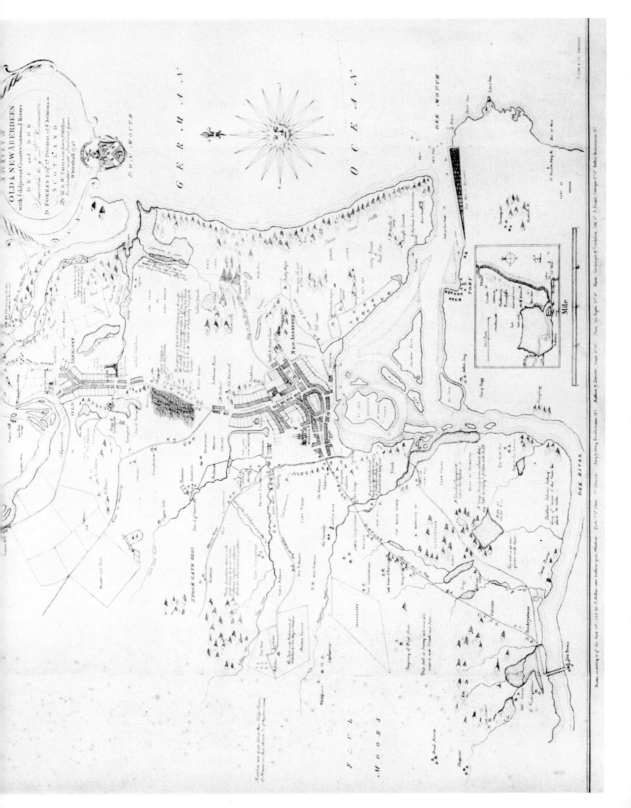

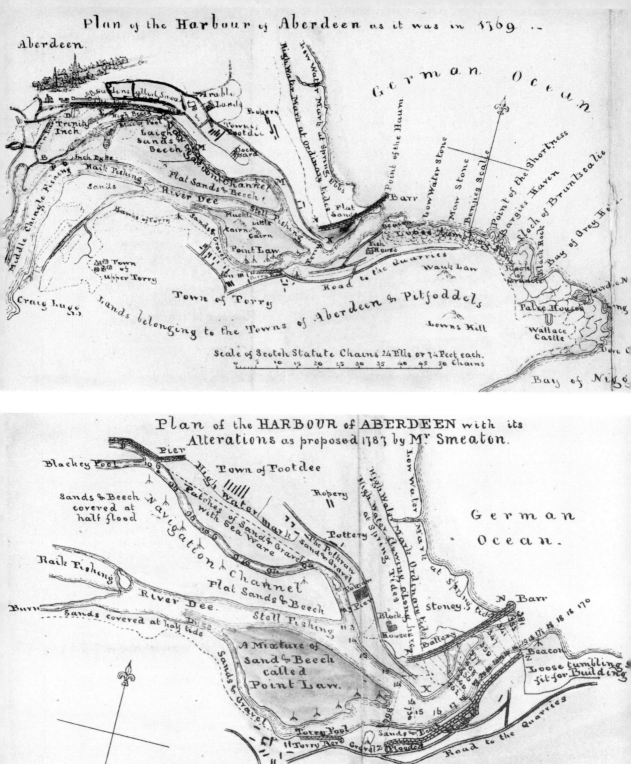

the north east, but few would have guessed that such an improvement would be achieved in the depth of the entrance. Smeaton was called back, and reported again in 1788. He advised construction of a spur jetty to act as a breakwater and wave trap, and this was built shortly afterwards. The first 1200 feet of the present North Pier is the original structure designed by Smeaton—a lasting memorial to a great engineer who paved the way for all subsequent developments of the harbour and the expanding trade of the city.

In the remaining years of the century the trade of the harbour rapidly increased to new record levels. Seven years after the completion of Smeaton's North Pier, annual figures showed some 165 ships used the harbour. By 1799, however, the number had grown to 1,759 ships with a tonnage of 104,480. An extract from the late-eighteenth century Statistical Account of Scotland (Table 3) shows a decline in foreign trade and fishing largely offset by increase in coastal trade.

Table 3

PORT OF ABERDEEN—An account of the total Number of Ships and Vessels, their Tonnage and Number of Men, belonging to this port, that traded to and from foreign Ports Coastwise, Fishing Smacks, &c. from 5th January 1787 to 5th January 1795, distinguishing each year.

Year ending	Foreign Trade			Coast Trade			Fishery		
	No of Vessels	Tons	Men	No of Vessels	Tons	Men	No of Vessels	Tons	Men
5th January 1788	63	4964	319	90	5520	396	12	1236	202
1789	64	5639	324	92	5675	350	8	1115	180
1790	69	5553	350	89	5811	334	12	1313	193
1791	73	5567	527	94	6578	853	12	1293	185
1792	44	3265	192	139	9417	673	7	1116	160
1793	48	3656	203	134	9200	673	11	1079	134
1794	37	3212	170	162	11126	869	11	998	121
1795	34	2984	165	168	11802	824	7	785	98

The origin and destination of the foreign trade is shown in Table 4.

facing page
8 Smeaton's plan of the Harbour 1769
9 Plan of Aberdeen with alterations proposed by Smeaton 1787

Records preserved in the Harbour Office, however, show foreign trade steadily increasing to the turn of the century with modest increases in coasting trade.

Smeaton's simple expedient of enhancing the natural scour of the river at the harbour entrance, and providing a barrier to the littoral southward drift of sand and shingle had been amply vindicated. With hindsight it is now all too easy to condemn the futility of constructing seventeenth century bulwarks on the south side of the channel.

Table 4

PORT OF ABERDEEN—An Account of the total Number of British and Foreign Ships, their Tonnage and Number of Men, including their repeated Voyages, that have entered at this Port, or cleared outwards to and from each foreign Kingdom or State, in the Year ending the 5th day of January 1795, showing the countries to which the foreign Vessels belong.

To or from what foreign kingdom or state	Countries to which foreign vessels belong	Inwards						Outwards					
		British			Foreign			British			Foreign		
		Ships	Tons	Men	Ships	Tons	Men	Ships	Tons	Men	Ships	Tons	Men
Granada	—	—	—	—	—	—	—	1	188	12	—	—	—
Denmark & Norway	Norway	15	875	49	11	890	64	6	334	18	1	100	6
Gibraltar	—	—	—	—	—	—	—	1	102	6	—	—	—
Greenland	—	3	653	85	—	—	—	3	653	85	—	—	—
Holland	—	14	1460	73	—	—	—	3	280	15	—	—	—
Ireland	—	1	88	5	—	—	—	—	—	—	—	—	—
Italy	—	—	—	—	—	—	—	1	90	6	—	—	—
Poland	—	4	343	20	—	—	—	—	—	—	—	—	—
Portugal	—	2	161	9	—	—	—	—	—	—	—	—	—
Germany	—	1	81	5	—	—	—	—	—	—	—	—	—
Prussia	—	4	870	34	1	60	5	1	243	9	—	—	—
Russia	—	8	803	44	—	—	—	6	796	42	—	—	—
Sweden	—	9	907	39	—	—	—	6	465	27	—	—	—
	Total	61	6041	363	12	950	69	28	3151	220	1	100	6

Strife and Progress

THE NINETEENTH CENTURY

There have been few periods in the long and interesting history of Aberdeen Harbour which have witnessed either such bitter conflict as occurred in the nineteenth century, or in which greater progress was made in harbour construction. Increased shipping demanded improved facilities, and the city fathers were besieged with advice and recommendation from all sides. On the one hand there were those wise and far-sighted citizens who forsaw the need to accommodate ever larger vessels, and to provide good quay facilities in which ships could lie afloat at all states of the tide. Inevitably, there were also those who foresaw that extensive harbour works would cost a great deal of money, and they feared the higher harbour charges. Sadly, there was a strong body of opinion amongst local businessmen who regarded themselves as experts in harbour construction, and from time to time they took it upon themselves to criticise some of the greatest civil engineers of the day, and substitute ill-conceived plans of their own. Fortunately, wise counsel eventually prevailed, the self-styled experts were cast aside, and the vast body of opinion which was opposed to any increase in rates and charges was overcome in the interest of progress. Mr Sargeant Merrywether, Counsel petitioning in May 1839 in favour of a Harbour Bill promoted by the Provost, Magistrates, and Town Council of Aberdeen, said in his opening speech:

> I never saw, when the greatest possible improvement was to be made, I never saw a case in which there would not be some people would rather that things should remain as they were, particularly if there was anything to be paid for it.

These wise words are as true today as they were long ago.

Despite bitter and fierce in-fighting between the protagonists, and with feeling running high in the city and surrounding countryside, the basis of the present harbour layout was developed. Some of the most remarkable works were executed with the most primitive of equipment, and the long life of these masonry structures has reflected much credit upon their designers and constructors. Although there were those amongst the city's manufacturers, shipowners, and merchants, who thought otherwise, Aberdeen was fortunate to benefit from the services of some of the greatest civil engineers of all time. John Smeaton, renowned as the builder of the great Eddystone Lighthouse and many of the greatest marine civil engineering works of his day, was the first to make any significant improvement upon the entrance to the harbour by his early construction of the first 1,200 feet of the North Pier which still stands to this very day. Thomas Telford, a famous builder of canals, bridges, and of harbours—extended the North Pier, commenced other major works, and laid down the basic plan to which the enclosed harbours were constructed in subsequent years. Around this time other great engineers, notably John Rennie, whose plan utilising a succession of groynes mercifully was not adopted, were also engaged to advise upon harbour design and construction work. These were followed by Walker, Abercromby and Abernethy, and by many other renowned experts in port construction.

10   Plan showing Harbour development proposed by Thomas Telford, 1802

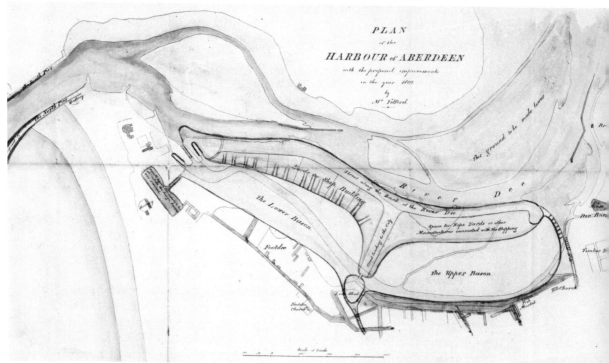

Smeaton's new North Pier described earlier fulfilled its purpose, and greatly improved the depth on the bar with consequent benefit to shipping. Problems arose, however, during easterly winds when the in-running swell was concentrated between Girdleness and the Pier, and entered the harbour freely with a disturbing effect on the shipping lying at anchor. Smeaton had been asked to return to Aberdeen, and in a second report dated 22 March 1778 he referred to his visits the previous October during the period of easterly winds, and freely admitted that he had not foreseen that the greatly increased depth in the Navigation Channel would also allow greater freedom for the easterly swells to enter the harbour. Despite the criticism of latter day commentators Smeaton was engaged specifically to improve the access to the harbour, and this he did to great effect constructing a pier under extremely difficult conditions with limited facilities, and with recourse only to manual labour. It was his very success in greatly improving access to the navigation channel that now allowed heavy swells the freedom to run into the harbour not previously possible.

Smeaton subsequently recommended the construction of a catch pier with a length up to 180 feet or thereby according to experience. This pier was to project into the navigation channel to minimise the effect of the inrunning swell, and he also recommended construction of the south pier.

Later, in 1797, John Rennie was engaged to study the harbour entrance with a view to making further improvements. Smeaton's works of 1778 had been most effective, but ships were still increasing in size, and with trade thriving, further works had become essential. Rennie remarked upon the fact that the improved entrance channel had now been scoured to a depth below the level of the foundations of Smeaton's north pier, and he suggested some improvements, but concurred with some of Smeaton's views about the erection of dykes. In essence, Rennie proposed the construction of a relatively small wet dock at Footdee which was to have been fed by the waters of the proposed Aberdeenshire canal. He then proposed a series of stone jetties at right angles to the main stream of the River which he argued would concentrate the waters of the Denburn and permit greater depths up to the Town Quays. The total cost of Rennie's scheme was estimated at £44,297 excluding the cost of purchase of land.

An Act for making and maintaining a navigable canal from the harbour in Aberdeen to Inverurie had received the Royal Assent in April 1796, and a further Act for enlarging and improving the harbour, for building new quays, wharves, and docks, and making various roads and passages had received the Royal Assent on 4 July 1797. Clearly Rennie's proposals necessitated the promotion of further Acts of Paliament, and the high cost of

11   The first Regent Bridge on Blaikies Quay (? date)

the works was daunting. The short comings of the scheme must have been apparent to the town fathers who baulked at the very high expense whereof the advantages were so patently limited. Had the scheme gone ahead as envisaged by Rennie, it seems doubtful if the harbour would have ever developed to any great extent, and as a consequence the whole development of the City of Aberdeen would have been permanently inhibited, and the course of history would have been very different.

Following further debate in the Town Council, Thomas Telford was instructed to draw up a plan of the improvements 'which appeared best calculated for perfecting the harbour and accommodating the trade of Aberdeen'. Telford, reporting on 29 April 1802 said:

> In forming this plan, I have been guided chiefly by the following considerations:
>
> 1st, to procure, at the least possible expense, the greatest expanse of space for wharfs and wet docks, or basins where vessels may lie afloat at low water.
>
> 2nd, to avoid injuring fisheries on the River Dee, on the south side, and occupying valuable ground on the north side, on those wet docks and basons.
>
> 3rd, to acquire new ground for shipbuilding, ropemaking, and, upon what are now mud banks along the north side of the Dee, and to provide proper communications from this new ground to the city and wharfs on the north side of the wet docks.
>
> 4th, to place the locks and graving docks upon the ground which affords the best foundations, and where they will be most conveniently situated for admitting vessels.
>
> 5th, to provide for scouring basins and entrances, space between the North and South Piers, and likewise the Bar.
>
> 6th, to procure and preserve four feet more water than there is on the Bar at present, in order to admit frigates and large merchantmen at high water neap tides.
>
> 7th, to form a proper connexion between the Canal and the Wet Docks.

Telford set about his work in the professional manner one would expect of the greatest harbour engineer of his day. Borings were made to test the sub-soil, and a very careful study was made. The report dated 28 April 1802 gave an approximate estimate of costs of £51,700. Whilst a little more expensive than the scheme proposed by Rennie, Telford's arrangements were altogether more cost-effective. A very much more detailed estimate was given

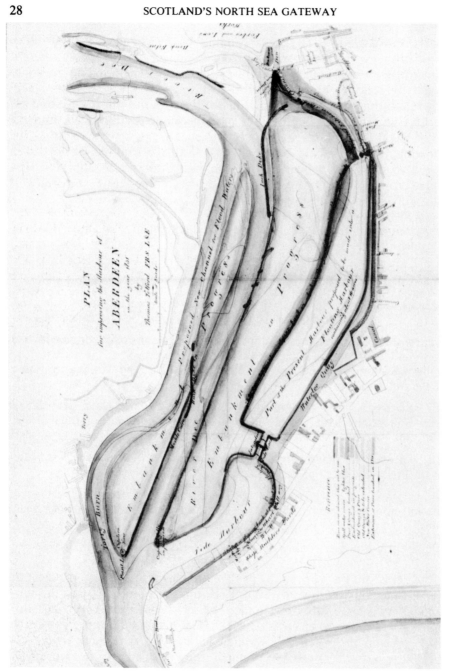

12 Telford's plan for Harbour improvement, 1831

in a subsequent report of 11 August 1809 with a revised total estimated cost of £121,913.

Telford's plan allowed for the construction of an enclosed dock, access locks, graving docks, construction of quays, and redirecting the main stream of the river. He proposed restoring the old south pierhead and extending the north and south piers, and he allowed for gates and a bridge across the dock opposite Commerce Street. On 18 May 1810, an Act was obtained by the City to amend their previous Acts for deepening and making more commodious the harbour. A further Act for improving the harbour was obtained on 22 June 1813 with yet another Act for harbour improvement receiving the Royal Assent on 14 May 1829.

Although there was a considerable diversity of opinion with regard to the plan for improving the interior of the harbour, all parties had agreed that the extension to the North Pier was essential. Within fifteen months of passing the 1810 Act, the North Pier was extended by an additional length of 300 feet, and this greatly improved the harbour entrance. It was then planned to extend the North Pier a further 600 feet—now into very much deeper water with exposure to the whole force of the North Sea. This work was of a far more serious nature, and enormous difficulties were encountered. A breakwater was constructed on the south side of the channel of some 800 feet

13 Harbour Mouth, 1838

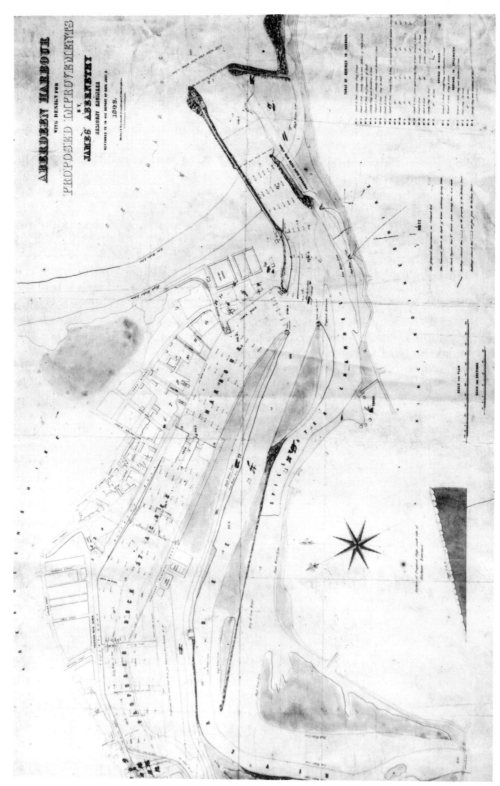

14 Plan of proposed Harbour developments and improvements by James Abernethy 1842

in length, but again some difficulties occurred in the construction, and by the time the two works were complete, extra expenditure of around £40,000 had been incurred beyond the original estimate for the entrance works. Improvements were made to the inner harbour and Waterloo Quay was constructed together with other works. Work was then held up for a period of eight years from 1817 when the City was in debt, and no capital work could be carried out, and only the most urgent of necessary repairs were put in hand.

Bitter criticisms of the City Council ensued, and there were strong moves to set up a new harbour constitution with Trustees representative of interests other than the Town Council. Self-styled experts were in full cry, and Telford was strongly criticised. These self-styled experts made irrelevant comparisons with the port of Dundee. At that port, harbour construction works had been carried out in sheltered water along the riverbank in quiet conditions which bore no comparison with those in Aberdeen. Dundee harbour dues were at that time less than Aberdeen, and many harbour users in Aberdeen bitterly resented the very high cost of works and the consequent rise in harbour charges. One Alexander Bannerman was perhaps the most bitter of Telford's opponents, describing Telford as obstinate and ignorant and his plans as 'ruinous and defective'; he accused Telford of blundering and the Magistrates of mismanagement.

In 1828 the magistrates and Council decided, in spite of opposition, to proceed with an application for a renewal of the Harbour Act in order to allow them to carry out further improvements. More bitter argument ensued, largely led by Alexander and Thomas Bannerman, again demanding that the magistrates and Council no longer be entrusted with the Trusteeship of the harbour, and that other interests be included as Harbour Trustees. Evidence was given to a Committee of the House of Commons at which petitions were heard from members of the Incorporated Trades, and by certain merchants, manufacturers, and shipowners. Evidence was also given by Robert Stephenson, various local shipmasters, and many others.

Eventually on 14 May 1829, the sixth Act was approved for harbour improvement. This repealed and consolidated previous Acts, and in deference to the many objectors provided that five Burgesses of Guild and one member of the Incorporated Trades join the Town Council as Trustees of the Harbour. The management of the harbour was thus delegated to a committee consisting of nine councillors and six outside elected members. Concessionary rates formerly enjoyed by the Burgesses of Guild and Members of the Incorporated Trades were largely withdrawn. Further quay construction was put in hand including a portion of Waterloo Quay, Trinity

Quay, Regent Quay, and Blaikies Quay. Extensive deepening operations were carried out, and the River Dee itself was both widened and deepened.

Although extensive works had been carried out to improve the harbour, deepen the channel and improve the access, etc, the wet dock contemplated in the Acts of 1810, 1813 and 1829 had not in fact been carried to a conclusion. Consequently, yet another Bill was laid before the House of Commons of which the main objective was the formation of the wet docks within the tidal harbour, The revised scheme was according to a plan by James Walker, President of the Society of Civil Engineers, and an expert in harbour construction. Following the death of Telford, Walker was considered to be without equal.

Inevitably, Walker's plan ran into opposition from yet more self-styled experts. Walker's plan was largely based on the original dock scheme devised by Telford, but contained a number of notable variations. An alternative plan was produced by three merchants and manufacturers, George Hogarth, Alexander Pirie, and William Reid. They, and their engineering contractor, proposed a different scheme which Walker regarded as both wild and impracticable. Other parties argued against the unfairness of the rates and charges, and others protested at the foul smells emanating from the harbour arising from the town sewers. Walker therefore proposed a new sewer, and an extension of the existing sewer with arrangements for scouring.

15 Harbour entrance, nineteenth century

This new Bill had been introduced by none other than Alexander Bannerman MP, one of those very same self-styled experts who had opposed previous efforts by the Town Council to improve the harbour! The second reading of this Bill took place on 15 April 1839, and twelve days later notice was given that the Bill would be heard in Committee on 6 May 1839. The Parliamentary Committee included Alexander Bannerman MP and Captain The Hon William Gordon MP, so both the city and the county were represented. Bannerman, having himself introduced the Bill, then appears to have taken sides with the objectors, and in a complete volte-face he proceeded to vote against his own Bill!

The Seventh Aberdeen Harbour Act eventually reached the statute books on 12 July 1843. This repealed the 1829 Statute, and vested the property of the harbour in a new body of Commissioners consisting of the magistrates and councillors, nine Burgesses of Guild, and three members of the Incorporated Trades. The Guildry and the Trades Commissioners all had to be holders of some property in lands or shipping. This Act contained powers to borrow some £270,000, and the Commissioners were authorised to proceed with the formation of Victoria Dock involving the construction of dock entrance works which would comprise a single entrance with lock gates. These were built between 1841 and 1848. Under this Act, further works were also carried out for the construction of Waterloo Quay East, Upper Quay, Blaikies Quay, and Matthews Quay. The harbour thus began to take on the outline of the present modern harbour of Aberdeen.

The Aberdeenshire Canal was first opened in 1807, and joined to the harbour by a sea lock in 1834. Mainly used for transport of coal, lime, and fertilisers, the canal was some 18¼ miles in length from Waterloo Quay to Port Elphinstone, near Inverurie. The canal cost some £44,000 to construct, and was 23 feet wide, 4 feet deep, and crossed by no less than 56 bridges. Fast gig boats carried passengers, and the Aberdeen Almanac of 1840 shows the vessels leaving Kittybrewster at 8 a.m. and returning from Port Elphinstone at 5 p.m. daily from 1 April to 15 September. Charges were 2s. 0d. (10p) in the fore-cabin, and 1s. 6d. (7½p) in the aft-cabin. Freight was carried from the Harbour to Inverurie in covered or open barges at a toll of ½d. to 2d. per ton per mile according to commodity. Unfortunately the Aberdeenshire Canal was not a financial success although it did contribute to the growing trade of the harbour. In 1853 the Canal was sold to the Great North of Scotland Railway Company, and much of the canal bed was used for laying the new railway track to the harbour area.

In 1847 power was granted to the Harbour Commissioners to sell ground located in the upper part of the inches and in the harbour to the Aberdeen

Railway Company. The Commissioners were, under the same Act, permitted to make certain alterations and introduce further new works connected with the harbour, and the revenue derived from the sale to the Railway Company was authorised for expenditure on these new habour works. The Act made provision also for the introduction of regulations for laying down of timber, and contained clarification as to the disposal of revenue derived from pilotage, metage, and weighing etc.

Progress in harbour development continued. In 1860, the first phase of Albert Quay construction was completed, and four years later a shed was erected at Waterloo Quay which was subsequently extended in 1868. That particular year became very important in harbour history due to a new Act which received Royal Assent on 13 July 1868. This Act again modified the constitution to provide for twelve elected Commissioners, and they were

16   Full rigged clipper ship, Victoria Dock, *c*.1890

required to serve with the Lord Provost and six Baillies, together with the Dean of Guild and eleven Councillors. This Act also made provision for the Harbour Commissioners to further extend the North Pier, to construct the South Breakwater, and to allow them to divert the course of the River Dee and make other harbour improvements. Harbour regulations were revised, and increased charges were authorised in order to offset debts and to pay for these extensive new works.

The new South Breakwater was constructed between 1869 and 1874, and the diversion of the River Dee was completed between 1870 and 1873. Many contemporary citizens do not realise that in fact the River Dee runs in an artificial canal constructed from the present Victoria Bridge to Point Law. The end of the old South Breakwater was removed between 1872 and 1880, and Albert Quay was further extended in 1873.

The days of strife and controversy were far from over. The third and final extension to the North Pier took place between 1874 and 1879, and the foundation stone was laid by HRH Prince Alfred, Duke of Edinburgh. Many were the opinions expressed as to how the protection of the harbour entrance should be executed. The eminent engineers Sir John Hawkshaw and James Abernethy had reported in October 1867 as to the recommended relative positions of the North Pier and South Breakwater, and following much controversy, and the expression of wide ranging opinions, they were called back to report upon proposals by the Harbour Engineer, William

17 Topsoil schooner entering Harbour after completion of the North Pier extension, *c.*1890

Dyce Cay, in 1876. In this last report Hawkshaw and Abernethy recommended the construction of a pitched slope from the Torry Harbour to the old South Breakwater to act as a half tide training wall. They also expressed the view that the North Pier should be further extended. It is of interest to note that this same report went on to say:

> As regard the discharge of the sewage at Abercromby's Jetty, there can be no doubt this is highly objectionable . . .

The very same discharge is still in use!

A wide variety of opinion had been expressed by shipowners, ships masters, the Captain Pilot, and by shipbuilders and others. The Harbour Engineer, Cay, subsequently recommended a further scheme whereby the River Dee would be diverted along a channel following closely the present high water mark on the south side of the entrance channel. He would thus

18   Construction of locks at Victoria Dock

19 Construction of locks at Victoria Dock

have left the main tidal harbour without any scouring effect other than the ebb and flow of the tide. If this scheme had been implemented, prolonged periods of easterly winds would have rendered the whole of the Victoria Dock inaccessible as a result of siltation, and the alternative would have been inordinately high dredging costs. Fortunately, the plan by Cay was never carried out, but further harbour works continued apace, with the construction of Jamiesons Quay, an extension to Albert Quay, and the deepening of the lock entrance and the lowering of the cill. The present Harbour Office was built between 1884 and 1886 at which time Matthews Cross Berth was also built.

In 1876 the harbour witnessed one of the worst disasters of the century when a ferry was swamped, and thirty-three passengers were drowned. The boat was hauled across the river from Torry to Point Law on a wire rope stretched across the river. The normal load for the boat was thirty persons, but the disaster occurred on a holiday and with sixty people crowded on board, their heavy weight tilted the craft in mid-stream, and the boat was swamped. At that time Wellington Bridge was the lowest crossing point. It would seem that this sad event stirred the authorities and Victoria Bridge was subsequently built and opened to traffic on 2 July 1881.

Additional borrowing powers were authorised in an Act of 1871 which provided for the purchase of the salmon fishings which had to be bought out from private proprietors in order to facilitate the digging of the artificial canal and redirection of the course of the River Dee. The Harbour Commissioners thus acquired the heritable rights which had been established by King Robert the Bruce in 1319, and which had previously passed from the ownership of the city into private hands. Additional improvements to the harbour, and provision of further quays necessitated the Commissioners seeking additional new powers to increase harbour charges and to borrow money. For this purpose an Act received the Royal Assent on 3 July 1879.

In 1887 another Act was obtained which confirmed an Order amending the earlier 1879 Act, and which allowed the Commissioners to take up further powers to apply new rates on goods and vessels, and to set aside quays for

20 Buoys in Upper Dock 1897; newly constructed Harbour Office in background

21 and 22 Construction of two-storey cargo shed, Regent Quay East, 1898

the landing of fish. This had become essential as a result of rapid growth in the fishing industry. In 1888 the lock cill was again deepened, a new gate was fitted, and the next year Pocra Lower Jetty was built and the east end of Commercial Quay was constructed. This latter quay was specifically required for the emergent fishing industry described in a later chapter.

The century was not closed without further rapid harbour development. Several more new quays were built—Palmerston Quay, Albert Quay Yawl Market, Commercial Quay West, Torry Harbour, Regent Quay East, and Regent Shed East. The old Regent Bridge was also replaced by a new swing bridge, and further extensions made to Albert Quay. The old pontoon dock had been installed in 1894, and a new face built at Upper Quay. All these works required further funds, and it was necessary to introduce a

23 Final stages of construction of two-storey cargo shed, Regent Quay East 1900

24 Cargo shed, Regent Quay East; top storey laid out for opening ceremony banquet, 1900

comprehensive Act which repealed previous legislation, re-affirmed the Board's constitution, and provided for the necessary increase in borrowing powers. The Act of 1895 permitted the Commissioners to increase their charges, and extended their powers to improve, maintain, administer and regulate the harbour. It was under this Act that the large programme of construction was initiated at the end of the century, but in the last few months of the century, yet another Act received the Royal Assent on 6 June 1899 which increased the Commissioners borrowing powers in order to allow them to finish off the works authorised by the 1895 Act.

To those unfamiliar with harbour history, the nineteenth century would thus seem a period of intense controversy, with frequent new legislation being promoted by the Harbour Commissioners in order to obtain funds for financing the harbour improvement. Nevertheless, in the space of 100 years,

25 Trinity Quay, Upper Dock, c.1890

26   sv *City of Aberdeen*, Upper Dock

the harbour changed from a few small riverside quays with very limited water depth, to a prosperous harbour little different in outline to that of the twentieth century harbour. During this period, the trade of the port increased beyond all recognition. Joseph Wood, Manager of the Aberdeen, Newcastle, and Hull Steam Company in 1876 complained that dues had been quadrupled in a period of fifty years. Against this, in 1799 some 1,759 ships of 104,480 tons used the harbour. In 1899 some 3368 commercial ships totalling 956,496 tons used the harbour, and almost 1¼ million tons of goods were handled through the port. The bitter strife to develop the harbour, was more than amply justified by the successful outcome. The century had opened with the nation at war with Napoleon. King George III occupied the throne, and Aberdeen was served by inadequate harbour facilities. It ended with the nation again at war, this time with the Boers in South Africa, Queen Victoria in her last years on the throne, and the new harbour of Aberdeen greatly prospering.

27 Topsail schooner under tow outward bound

THE TWENTIETH CENTURY

And so to the twentieth century. Another era of great change in the fortunes and the development of the harbour, but a time in which changes were wrought over a much shorter term than in any other time of development activity. For the first time, the port had to face the competition of other major Scottish east coast ports and harbours, and indeed of ports in England.

The first year of the twentieth century showed a profit resulting from a surplus of revenue over expenditure of £15,081.19s. 6d. The century had, however, commenced with the Harbour Commissioners facing liabilities of some £422,098.16s. 3d., but traffic levels were fairly high with a little short of 1¼ million tons of cargo being handled exclusive of fish. Imports predominated, the traffic was handled by some 3,391 ship arrivals—mostly in the coastwise trade. Some 45,563 tons of fish were landed by some 7,575 trawler arrivals, 1,941 steam line vessel arrivals, and 8,357 sail line vessels.

28   Barquentine under tow entering Harbour, c.1908

29   Construction of an early cargo transit shed at Regent Quay West 1902

30   Regent Quay showing Harbour Office and a cargo of timber stacked ready for delivery,
     c.1900

The Commissioners' salmon fishing showed a profit of £1,943 and present day loss making activities such as cranage and metage (tallying etc) were all profitable. With trade so buoyant, it only remained for the Commissioners to tackle the very heavy burden of debt.

Although the harbour layout, by the turn of the century, largely corresponded to its present day form, nevertheless substantial improvement works were urgently required. Any ideas that the Commissioners had of wiping the slate clean of their capital debt were, therefore, largely doomed to failure. In 1901, Matthews Quay was constructed, and a new face was built across Palmerston Quay. The year following, Regent Shed West was constructed, and works were commenced on the widening of Commercial Quay. In 1903 work commenced on the construction of Torry Quay adjacent to the siphon house and tanker terminal, and at the same time work was initiated for the widening of Regent Quay East, and Point Law was removed.

31　Harbour Commissioners inspecting new works at Torry, 1904

Most harbour users today are unaware that originally Point Law extended to a point far beyond the present Point Law Cross Quay, and work extended over some four years to completely remove the structure and to construct the Cross Quay. Over the next ten years, Pocra Quay was improved, Mearns Quay constructed, Point Law Cross Berth was completed, a new face built at Blaikies Quay, and Regent Shed East was widened.

A new Regent Quay swing bridge across the entrance to Upper Dock was opened on 29 August 1904 by the wife of the Lord Provost. The new bridge powered by hydraulic machinery replaced an old hand operated bridge, and the entrance was widened to admit access to Upper Dock by larger vessels. The first ship to pass through was s.s. *Spray*, a well-known Aberdeen collier, which was gaily decorated for the occasion.

Major works were commenced in 1909 for the construction of River Dee Dock. This provided three new quays, and was originally intended for the

32   Commencement of the construction of River Dee Dock, 1909

33 Road Bridge and lock gates at Jamieson Quay, c.1910

fishing industry. Work was completed in 1915 just after the outset of World War I.

The harbour facilities were not ignored by the Commissioners. In 1910 sheerlegs were built adjoining the North Lock, and this was of paramount importance for local shipbuilders in helping installation of heavy machinery into new ships, and in particular was used for installing boilers and main engines. the sheerlegs were also available for the handling of cargo, but proved somewhat slow in operation. For ship repairs, Pontoon Dock No 1 came into use in 1911, and the following year work commenced on building a new quay front at the yawl market at Albert Quay West.

Just as the new Pontoon Dock No 1 entered service, so the older graving dock was closed two years later in 1913. Temporarily re-opened during World War I, this important ship repairing facility was finally removed between 1924 and 1927.

34 Graving Dock at Point Law, built in 1882–6 and closed 1915

As indicated in a later chapter, World War I was not an easy time for the port or for port users. The Commissioners were limited in their ability to continue the process of improvement, but between 1914 and 1917 substantial improvements were carried out to Waterloo Quay West, and between 1914 and 1923 a further section of Mearns Quay was constructed. At the end of the War the seaward North Lock Gates were closed having only been in use once in 1916 and once in 1917. The east gates were left permanently open to give access to the sheer poles, and eventually the whole lock was infilled and a new berth created in Victoria Dock in 1981.

With the arrival of Peace in 1918, the Commissioners gave consideration to the further improvement of their habour. In the five year period commencing 1923, the entrance channel was deepened to 34 feet in order to accommodate the rapidly increasing size of ships using the port. There would have been little point in improving quay facilities if the port had become inaccessible to the larger type of vessel. Following completion of this deepening work, Pacific Wharf was constructed providing a good deep water quay with open surface ideally suited to the handling of bulk cargoes.

35   Construction work at Waterloo Quay, 1914

During the years of depression in the late 1920s and early 1930s, Aberdeen Harbour suffered less than most. The Commissioners were able to reconstruct the face of Commercial Quay, they removed Pocra Lower Jetty, and reconstructed the face of Trinity Quay. Immediately before World War II broke out, the Harbour Commissioners commenced the major work of widening of the new South Breakwater. This was a difficult task necessitating the movement of vast quantities of material and the placing of huge blocks of masonry for which a special crane had to be employed. The work was not finally completed until 1965.

In 1939 Matthews Quay Cross Berth was improved to provide better facilities for the North Boats which traded regularly to Shetland and Orkney. During the war years which followed, very little work could be carried out to further improve the harbour which was soon in the front line facing enemy occupied coasts, and constantly under the threat of invasion. Work was, however, put in hand between 1942 and 1943 for the renovation of Jamiesons Quay, and in 1945 the lock cill was deepened. At the end of the war the barbed wire fences, military installations, boom defence, air-raid shelters and all other panoply of war all had to be removed.

36 Dredgers at work deepening the Harbour

Following the cessation of hostilities, like most public authorities, and indeed like the Corporation of the City of Aberdeen, the Harbour Commissioners addressed themselves to developing plans for post-war improvement. The first scheme to be put in hand was the construction of Atlantic Wharf between 1946 and 1949, and in 1949 a two storey transit shed was built at this second deep water berth. In 1947 the North Lock outer gate was finally sealed following the improvement two years earlier to the main lock. The Point Law oil terminal was developed in the period 1948–51, and between 1950 and 1953 further improvements were carried out to the locks including the provision of a new bascule lifting bridge which was opened by HM Queen Elizabeth the Queen Mother on 30 September 1953. At the same time Albert Quay face was further improved and modernised, the old pontoon dock was replaced, and a new leading jetty was constructed adjoining the locks.

In 1955 the Regent Oil Company, forerunners of Texaco, constructed their quay in the River Dee along with their oil distribution depot. Three years later Matthews Quay was refaced, and in 1960 the large No 1 Pontoon Dock was finally removed.

It can therefore be seen that throughout the first half of the twentieth century, the Commissioners had been diligent in their upkeep of the facilities of the Harbour, and in installing new cranes and in improving their quays and transit sheds. The old constitution with thirty Board members was, however, clearly unwieldy and outdated despite having worked adequately

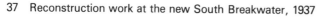

37   Reconstruction work at the new South Breakwater, 1937

38 and 39 Steam lorry used during construction works at the new South Breakwater

over a long period of time since 1868. After extensive discussions, a new constitution was evolved whereby the Board was to comprise a reduced number of members consisting of:

2 members appointed by the Aberdeen Chamber of Commerce
2 members appointed by the Scottish Trades Union Congress
4 members appointed by the Corporation of the City of Aberdeen
7 members elected by harbour users, by Burgesses of Guild, and by Members
  of the Incorporated Trades along very similar lines to the electoral procedure
  which had subsisted since the 19th century.

Surprisingly the change in Board membership, which took effect from 1 January 1961 when the Aberdeen Harbour Order Confirmation Act 1960 came into force, made no provision for senior professional members of the Board staff to be executive directors. The Board's chief executive, the General Manager, however, continued to play a major role at all Board meetings. The same constitution continues to this day, except that, following Local Government reorganisation in 1975, Grampian Regional Council appoint four members to the Board instead of the City Council. Following the recommendation of the National Ports Council, there was a serious attempt to make a further change in 1973–4. This attracted strong objections, and was eventually quashed by Parliamentary Commissioners at a public inquiry. The matter has subsequently been considered on two separate occasions by the Harbour Board, but the constitution still differs from all other major ports in Britain in that no senior executive or professional officer is a member. Notwithstanding this, the Board has worked remarkably well, but this is perhaps attributable to the first class individual members, to the zeal with which they have pursued the Board's interests and those of the harbour, and above all to the very close co-operation which has always existed between Board members and the senior management. The success of the port is thus attributable to the quality of individual board members and management, rather than to the system by which the Board is constituted.

The newly constituted Board of 1961 very quickly addressed itself to further harbour improvement, and inherited a very considerable responsibility in attracting new business, providing improved facilities for the existing trade, and in facing up to the enormous technological change in cargo handling and indeed in all aspects of shipping. The nineteenth century undoubtedly saw the greatest period of overall change in the harbour, but the three decades following the reconstitution of the Board in 1960 were without

Table 5 ABERDEEN HARBOUR BOARD

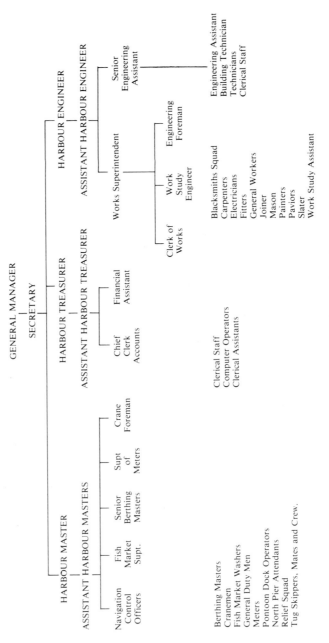

GENERAL MANAGER
SECRETARY

HARBOUR MASTER — HARBOUR TREASURER — HARBOUR ENGINEER

ASSISTANT HARBOUR MASTERS

- Navigation Control Officers
- Fish Market Supt.
- Senior Berthing Masters
- Supt of Meters
- Crane Foreman

Berthing Masters
Cranemen
Fish Market Washers
General Duty Men
Meters
Pontoon Dock Operators
North Pier Attendants
Relief Squad
Tug Skippers, Mates and Crew.

ASSISTANT HARBOUR TREASURER

- Chief Clerk Accounts
- Financial Assistant

Clerical Staff
Computer Operators
Clerical Assistants

ASSISTANT HARBOUR ENGINEER

- Works Superintendent
- Senior Engineering Assistant

Clerk of Works — Work Study Engineer — Engineering Foreman

Blacksmiths Squad
Carpenters
Electricians
Fitters
General Workers
Joiner
Mason
Painters
Paviors
Slater
Work Study Assistant

Engineering Assistant
Building Technician
Technicians
Clerical Staff

N.B. This chart shows the pattern of organisation only, and does not purport to reflect exact seniority or rank.

question the most intense and concentrated period of harbour improvement in the very long history of the port.

Upon taking office, the new Board put in hand the reconstruction of the face of Upper Quay, and in 1962 the Point Law coaling installation was removed after only fourteen years in operation. The change from coal to oil powered vessels foreshadowed the demise of coal bunker trade, and there was a drastic fall in coal imports concurrently. In 1963 the old Waterloo shed, being wholly unsuited to modern cargo handling, was removed and for similar reasons Regent Shed West was removed the year following. In 1964 the herring market was built at Mearns Quay, but this too had a very short life as it had to be withdrawn from service when the old quay became unserviceable early in the next decade.

Pocra Quay was further improved along its faceline in 1965, but this was in effect only a short term measure, and the whole quay had to be completely rebuilt in 1983. In the same year, 1965–6, Pacific Wharf was refaced and the berth deepened, and the former transit shed at that point was removed.

In 1966 the Round House, the port navigation control centre originally built about 150 years earlier, and situated at the foot of the North Pier was heightened, but the Commissioners were careful to preserve the integrity of the appearance of the old building. Subsequently, all the operating controls, fog signals, navigation lights, and the port's VHF radio were installed in a console in the Round House, and improvements were carried out to the interior of the building. Then, in the early 1970s, navigation control radar was installed to facilitate the movement of ships, and enhance shipping control.

The fish markets had continued to be owned and operated by Aberdeen Corporation, even after reconstitution of the Board. Following prolonged negotiation, all the fish markets—now in poor repair—were acquired by the Harbour Board at a cost of £37,500. Before the sale was complete, some 600 feet of decayed fish market at the east end of Commercial Quay had to be withdrawn from use due to collapse, and the Board quickly set about preparing replacement plans and investigating ways and means of introducing mechanical fish handling systems.

Further works and improvement were carried out over the next few years, but when the Board granted a lease to Shell UK Exploration and Production for land at Torry on 28 May 1965, important events for Aberdeen Harbour were fore-shadowed. In 1969 the first drilling mud silos were erected along with cement silos, and the harbour suddenly found itself in the forefront of North Sea oil exploration activities. Seismic survey vessels had been a common sight in the harbour before this, but from this point onwards the pace began to increase.

British ports by tradition had generally operated on the basis of normal working hours 8 a.m. to 5 p.m. Those ports, such as Aberdeen, who were engaged in the fishing industry had a tradition of working unusual hours in order to land fish, and thus conditioned, Aberdeen was probably in a better position to face the demands of the emergent oil industry who now demanded a twenty-four hour service.

It has to be remembered that all this time the entrance to Upper and Victoria Dock was controlled by lock gates which only gave access from two to three hours before high tide to a similar period after high tide. Clearly this was no use to an industry demanding a 365 day a year operation on a twenty-four hour basis. Like King Canute, Aberdeen Harbour Board, could not control tides, and they could, and indeed they did, promptly set about converting the port into a twenty-four hour availability.

Blaikies Quay was the first quay to be completely reconstructed, but sadly some of the old quays in the fishing sector of the harbour in Albert Basin had already exceeded their economic life and soon began to fail. As previously mentioned, a section of 600 feet at the west end of Commercial Quay was the first to collapse, and serious problems ensued. The fishing industry was deprived of important berthing facilities, and the Harbour Board found themselves in a dilemma in having to completely reconstruct both quay and market buildings despite shortage of sufficient funds. With the aid of government grant facilities amounting to 20 per cent of the cost, made available by the Department of Agriculture and Fisheries for Scotland, work was put in hand in 1969 and a new fish market building was erected. This building had only been in use a year or two when Palmerston Quay failed, and following collision by a fishing vessel had to be withdrawn from use. An examination of Albert Quay and Commercial Quay West showed those quays also to be in poor condition and since fish landings were at that time relatively heavy, the Board were forced to take action.

Traditionally in British ports, fishing vessels have generally enjoyed privileged rates of ships dues and charges. Aberdeen was no exception, and insufficient revenue was being generated by the industry to pay for new facilities. A long round of negotiations began with a view to obtaining grant aid, and eventually after interminable arguments as to the design, and in spite of great difficulties encountered in attempting to persuade the National Ports Council and Department of Transport officials that the project was viable, the government made available a 60 per cent grant, and work was put in hand for the reconstruction of Albert Quay and Palmerston Quay. Both quays were to be provided with a single storey fish market building of greatly improved design, but sadly not on the grand scale envisaged by the Harbour

Board, and which would have been similar to the new fish markets then being provided at major continental fishing ports.

Whilst all this was proceeding, Blaikies Quay reconstruction had been completed, and the Board were intent upon providing twenty-four hour access to the enclosed docks. Clearly, had the lock gates been opened and all the quays exposed to tidal action, hydrostatic pressures would have built up behind the older quays which would then have collapsed. Every quay in the enclosed docks had to be rebuilt, but a flying start had been given by the earlier completion of Blaikies Quay. Trinity Quay, and Upper Quay were both rebuilt and work was put in hand for the reconstruction of Waterloo Quay. By this time offshore supply vessels were regularly using the harbour, and the Board's officials had diligently researched the needs of the oil industry and were now attempting to provide facilities at their fastest speed, but unhappily the industry was developing even faster. At one stage, a particularly large number of quays had been taken out of service for reconstruction, and harbour congestion became severe for a short period. One school of thought suggested that the Board had perhaps tried to do too much too soon, but their decisions were soon proved extremely wise since the port was soon able to offer surplus berthing facilities.

40   Modern Turkish bulk cargo vessel at Waterloo Quay

It has to be remembered that all these works made enormous demands upon the Board's fairly limited financial resources. Not one penny of government grant aid was proferred toward reconstruction for the emergent offshore industry. Indeed, both government and National Ports Council refused to accept the optimistic views of Aberdeen Harbour Board. The Board's own assessment of the rate of development, and of demand for berthing facilities, were eventually proved to be infinitely more accurate than government assessments. Borrowing money presented a major obstacle. It has to be remembered that the ports of London and Liverpool were in acute financial distress at this particular point in time, and the financial institutions were in no mood to make loans available to port authorities. The Board's Chairman, Roger Fleming, and General Manager, Norman Beattie, strove valiantly to obtain reasonable loan facilities, but in the end recourse had to be made to government loans provided under Section 11 of the Harbours Act, 1964. High rates of interest obtained, and at one particular stage the British government was making loan money available at an interest rate of 14¼ per cent at a time when Norwegian ports were borrowing from their government for similar purposes at around 6½ per cent, and Dutch ports at little more. Before the government would make any loan facilities available, stringent financial criteria had to be satisfied, and long and hard were the many debates which took place. The end result was a happy one for Aberdeen, and although vast sums of interest had to be serviced from port revenue, sufficient loan facilities were eventually made available for the vast reconstruction works to be put in hand.

With the reconstruction of the quays in the enclosed docks completed, the lock gates could be removed. Sadly, the underwater shape of the locks was a 'U' form, to match the underwater hull form of sailing ships. Modern ships were, however, square in cross section, and only the smaller vessels could gain access at all states of the tide. The whole lock entrance, therefore, had to be removed, and all the old battles with government were re-opened in order to obtain permission for the Board to spend its own money—without any form of grant aid or loan—to undertake the work. Fortuitously, however, at this particular time grant aid did become available unexpectedly from the EEC Regional Development Fund.

Details of EEC fund facilities, and of arrangements for claiming grant aid were received one morning in the post at 08.30 a.m. All other management work came to a standstill, and in less than one hour the formal application was in the post seeking aid for the lock entrance. Happily, the effort was not in vain, and Aberdeen was included amongst the very first ports in Britain to receive aid from this source achieving no less than 30 per cent of the cost of widening and deepening the lock entrance. Subsequently, aid was obtained from this source for a number of other facilities in the harbour before the North East of Scotland lost development area status, and thus forfeited financial aid from the EEC.

With new developments in cargo handling, the port had to keep pace in terms of handling equipment. A new 50 tonne capacity heavy lift crane was erected at Pacific Wharf which has a capability of handling international standard shipping containers. At the same time, the old sheerlegs at the North Lock were removed. Again, the ferry services to the Northern Isles, then operated by the North of Scotland Orkney and Shetland Shipping Company Limited, came under economic pressure to change the laborious methods of loading their ships, and discussions commenced with the Harbour Board with a view to providing drive-on/drive-off—commonly known as 'ro-ro'—facilities. After extensive discussion, and with the full co-operation of the Scottish Office who made modest grant aid available in order to help the island communities, new facilities were constructed at Jamiesons Quay. A modern passenger terminal was built together with associated offices, new lairages were built for livestock, and a large transit shed was constructed for assembly of outward cargoes and for the sorting of inward cargoes prior to despatch to inland destinations. The new service was initiated by the passenger/car/freight ferry *St Clair*, and this was later augmented by *St Magnus*, a freight only ferry with limited passenger accommodation.

With the advent of the ro-ro cargo handling technique, the Board clearly had to provide additional separate facilities for international ro-ro traffic. Very heavy lifts carried by this type of vessel had previously been handled in the harbour, but they could only be handled at certain states of the tide, and only at one particular corner of Waterloo Quay strengthened for the purpose. The Board's officials therefore set about a detailed programme of research to find the most suitable equipment. For convenience and cost reasons, most ports utilise the corner of a dock for a fixed ramp, but this was clearly impossible for Aberdeen, and the first firms approached with a view to specialised construction disdained the Board's management proposals and claimed them to be unworkable. Nevertheless, a first class design was evolved, and further development took place in close association with the Finnish company, Navire. In due course an invitation to tender was sent out and both British and foreign companies were invited to submit design proposals. Navire offered the cheapest price, the best design, and the shortest construction period, and the new 'Aberdeen Eurolink' was completed in April 1979 when a naming ceremony was held in

41   Reconstruction of Mearns Quay East

42   Reconstruction of Mearns Quay West, River Dee, November 1983

Finland—attended by the only Finnish exponent of the bagpipes who spoke not one word of the English language! The floating ramp was delivered by sea to Aberdeen, and can now be used at almost any quay in the harbour, and can be moved within one to two hours. The original design was unique, but has now been copied in many parts of the world by many manufacturers.

On 1 April 1978 the last remaining section of the fish market, Commercial Quay West, deteriorated further and having become dangerous had to be withdrawn from service at short notice. This caused immense difficulty for the fishing industry, and after interminable wrangling with government officials who foresaw no future for the fishing industry, limited grant aid of 20 per cent of the cost was eventually made available. The Board then sought grant aid from the European Community, but were advised by British government departments that only limited aid was available for the relatively inexpensive fish market buildings, and the costly quay was ineligible for any form of European grant aid. Persistence won the day, however, and after several visits to Brussels, and careful investigation of community rules, further grant aid was obtained for the quay construction works amounting to 30 per cent of the total cost—this worth a little over £¾ million, and well worth the effort which had gone before.

The Harbour Board, never content to rest upon their laurels, continued to make progress in their aim of continual harbour improvement. A mammoth task was commenced to replace all the harbour roadways, and this is now largely complete. All the quays in the River Dee on the north side have been completely rebuilt, and this has provided a new tanker terminal for BP Oils Limited, a new quay for fishing vessels, and the port's ninth oil base. There is still further space in the River Dee for further development of additional small quays. Point Law Cross Berth, to which previous reference has been made, has been completely reconstructed following the appearance of huge structural cracks caused by harbour dredging. The old north abutment for the former Regent swingbridge has been removed, and the old transit shed on Regent Quay which had stood for sixty years and had become completely sterile and useless for modern cargo handling was removed. Two new deep water berths were constructed, and two new transit sheds specifically adapted for the handling of forest products have been built. Huge modern cranes have been installed, and indeed the whole of the Board's crane fleet has been replaced since the war. The mobile cranes include some of the most advanced types in the world—all with very heavy lifting capacity, and some capable of lifting 80 tons.

The Board continues to look to the future. Over the next ten years, there are plans for expenditure in the order of £30 million for major maintenance, and improvement of the harbour. Considerable research has been undertaken into future trading trends, and studies have been carried out to see how additional port facilities can be provided should the need arise. In short, the incredible changes which have been wrought in the latter part of the twentieth century have created an acute awareness of change, and new technologies are under constant examination in order to see how further harbour improvements can be effected in advance of actual requirement. Where once the former Harbour Commissioners set about the provision of facilities in consequence of change, the present management and Harbour Board try to adopt a philosophy of anticipating change in order to remain ahead of the field. This can be attributed to an enlightened Board, to the development of highly specialised professional port management, and to loyal conscientious staff. This compares with the sparse management in the previous century, and policies determined by a large and unwieldy body of Harbour Commissioners.

43 Regent Quay 1985. Replacement of old timber quay by new sheet steel piling quay to provide deep water berthing for large ships.

Navigation and Pilotage

The clear unobstructed approach to the present day Aberdeen harbour, the fine well-protected entrance, and the deep water available at all states of the tide within the harbour, together make it very difficult to visualise the difficult access to the estuary of the Dee in bygone days. When the famous eighteenth century engineer, John Smeaton, was appointed to report upon the harbour in 1769, the entrance had in fact changed little from earliest times. Maps from the seventeenth century differed but little from those of the eighteenth century, and access to shipping was extremely difficult. Geologically, the estuary of the River Dee comprises a hollow in the glacial drift, is about a mile and a half in length east to west, and about half a mile across, filled with alluvial beds of gravel, clay, and fine sand. On the south side, Girdleness, a rocky promontory projects half a mile beyond the mouth of the river, and is connected with the mainland by a hill of drift sand, thus forming a natural protection to the harbour. On the north side, however, the coast is low and covered with beach sand.

The earliest written description of the harbour approaches from the sea is that by Philopoliteius writing in 1658 *A Succint Survey of the City of Aberdeen*. This was printed by John Forbes in Aberdeen in the same year, and gives the following sailing directions:

> A ship coming from the south, bound for the road and harbour of Aberdeen, a mile to the southward of the road, ye will see a bay with a country church standing in the middle thereof, called the Kirk of Nigg; to the northward lyeth the Girdle-nes (or Aberdeen-nes) which when ye come bye come no nearer the same than a long cable length, and as soon as ye come by it, you will see two sharp spire steeples, which steeples ye must run to the northward untill ye open the west-most steeple a sailes' breadth to the northward of the eastmost, and there ye may anchor on 9 or 10 fathom water, where ye may tide with northerly, southerly, or westerly winds. As for the harbour, at the entrie thereof is a Barr. Whereon at low water there is scarce on it 2 foot water; on the south side of the Barr, there stands a Beackon which in the incoming ye must leave on your larboard-side a ship's breadth free thereof, where commonly the best of the channell doeth run. From the Beackon to the eastward even to the

Girdle-nes is all rocks. At the spring-tydes, there will be thereon about 15 foot water, at neep tydes no more than about 9 or 10 foot. But I shall not advise a stranger to seek that harbour without a pilot; because it is a pilots fairway: and as soon as ye come to the Road ye can allwayes have a boat for putting out a Vaisse at all occasions, for piloting you into the harbour. The nearest rake of the said harbour is north east and south west, and when ye are within the said harbour ye lye landlocked for all winds, but at low water, your ships lye dry and very good ground.

In 1682 Captain Greenville Collins was appointed by King Charles II to survey the coast of Great Britain there being at that time 'no sea charter or maps of these kingdoms but what were Dutch or copies from them and these very erroneous'. Captain Collins was an officer in the Royal Navy and a younger brother of Trinity House. His work took some seven years. The individual charts were issued as they were completed, and of course subsequently there were many printings. The first collected edition was published in 1693 under the title *Great Britain's Coasting Pilot* and was the first complete pilot book in English of the British coast. Of Aberdeen and the approaches, Captain Collins is less than happy. He writes:

Girdlenais. From Dounfit to Girdlenais the Course is NNE. half E. 4 Leagues. A little to the Northward of Girdlenais is the Bay of Aberdeen, where is good Anchoring in 7, 8 or 9 Fathom Water; you may bring the Point of Girdlenais S. and S. by E.

Aberdeen. Lieth a Mile to the Westward of Girdlenais, and is a Tide Haven, where Vessels enter at High-water; you sail close in by the South Shore: the Entrance into the River is very narrow. On the Larboard-side, going in, is a Beacon which sail close by; the North Shore is a low sandy Point on which is a Block-house, which you leave on the Starboard-side. You must not venture in here without a Pilot. for the Bar often alters: And you are observe, that no Ship of any Burthen, that draws 10, 11 or 12 Foot Water, will adventure here, but when the Water is very smooth and the Winds offshore, and Spring Tides. Here are always Boats ready to help Ships in and out.

Buchannais. From Girdlenais to Buchannais, the Course is NNE. and NE. by N. eight or nine Leagues. In the Midway between them is Newbrough Creek, a place only for small Vessels."

The account contained in the first report by John Smeaton dated 19 February 1770 (reprinted in full in the Appendix) gives a much more detailed picture of the original harbour and its entrance.

The first navigation aids for the guidance of mariners appear to have been

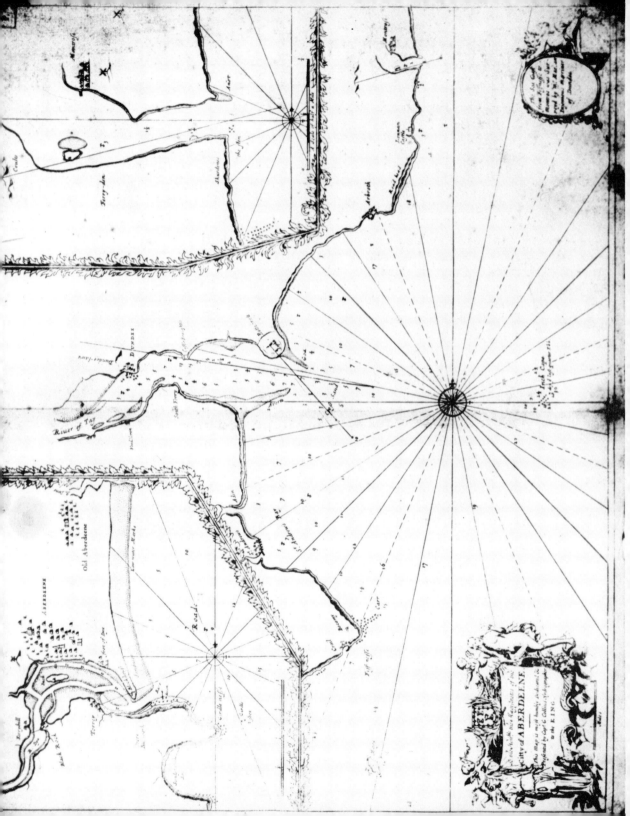

beacons erected around the year 1484. In 1511 a number of municipal statutes laid down marine regulations for ships to lie in the 'Gawpuyl', and these were augmented by further regulations in 1542—'in which year lykewayes the mouth of the Dee was locked with chains of irone and masts of ships crossing the river not to be opened bot at the citizens pleasure.' Further regulations were laid down in 1561 which included instructions to prevent the dumping of ballast within the flood mark. About this time, in 1556, the first lighthouse came into being erected on the east gable of the Chapel of St Ninian on the Castle Hill. Three new beacons were built in 1597, the first two being erected on 12 and 13 September respectively. A contemporary description was of 'ane gryt bowet, with thrie flamying lichts'. Erection of these beacons appears to have been thirsty work since a significant item in the surviving account provides for drinks for the workmen. One of these beacons appears to have been erected on 'Chappell Hill' which we must presume to be the former Castle Hill probably in the vicinity of St Ninian's Chapel.

It was the 1596 Charter of King James VI which marks the first real attempt to improve the harbour entrance and the navigation channel. By this Charter, the magistrates were empowered to raise charges on vessels using the harbour, and these revenues were to be deployed in harbour improvements. Detailed records are still preserved in Aberdeen in the Charter Room of the Town House, and they throw an interesting light upon both the trade of the harbour and the improvements carried out.

It has to be said that some of the improvements were well-intentioned, but of very limited use, the most notable of these being the construction of the bulwark between 1607 and 1608. This was erected on the south side of the channel with the intention of concentrating the stream of the river with a view to creating a scouring action thus deepening the channel over the bar. Of course it failed to do this, and as early reports showed, entrance to the harbour was difficult in the extreme. Had the citizens expended their efforts to construct a pier on the north side, their efforts may have produced some better results by retaining the sand of the Sand-ness, and effectively concentrating the channel—there being rock to the south which would not be eroded. About this time, a huge boulder called Craig Metellan or the Maitland Rock, lay in the fairway creating a hazard to ships entering or leaving the Harbour. It was imperative that this be removed if the trade was to be encouraged, and the Town Council offered a fee of 300 merks

facing page

44   Chart prepared by Captain Greenville Collins, 1682 of approaches to Aberdeen Harbour (*top left*), Dundee Harbour (*centre*), and Montrose Harbour (*top right*)

(approximately £17) for shifting the stone. David Anderson of Finzeauch ('Davie do a'thing') first measured the rise and fall of the tide, fifteen feet at the springs and ten feet at the neaps; he then attached a number of empty barrels to the rock at low water so that the buoyancy derived from the barrels on the flooding tide lifted the stone. Anderson was then able to float it up channel, steering in to the bank well clear of the navigation channel.

The Aberdeen Shipmasters Society founded in 1598, and granted a Charter by King James VI on 19 February 1600, did much to persuade the Town Council to improve the harbour. Originally set up as a charitable institution to make provision for their colleagues in distress, the Society also formed a very important professional pressure group, and constantly addressed the magistrates with a view to effecting improvements to the navigation of the port. Then, as in the nineteenth century and even today, there was no shortage of self-styled experts on port and harbour operation, construction, and administration. The Shipmasters, however, were professionals and did have the advantage of both knowledge of navigation, and practical experience in harbour usage. The Society, one of the earliest incorporations in Aberdeen, was still acting as a professional pressure group as recently as 1813 when, following the sad loss of the whaler *Oscar*, their advocacy of erection of a lighthouse at Girdleness provided the necessary stimulus for the Town Council, who in turn, persuaded the Commissioners of Northern Lighthouses to erect the lighthouse at Girdleness. Shortly after the reconstitution of the Shipmasters Society in 1801, at the request of the Harbour Trustees, the Society undertook the examination of pilots. These examinations were held in January each year and took place in either the Society's Hall or the Town House. This valuable work continued until the passing of a new Act in 1839 when they ceased to carry out this important duty.

Girdleness lighthouse was finally completed in 1833. Lighthouses had earlier been constructed at Kinnaird Head in 1787 and at Buchanness in 1827. Lighthouses were later erected at Scurdie Ness in the approaches to Montrose Harbour in 1870, and at Rattray Head in 1895. Todhead lighthouse to the south of Aberdeen was constructed in 1897. All these lighthouses continue in use, but they have been greatly changed and improved from those early days. The Commissioners of Northern Lighthouses were the pioneers in Britain of using high efficiency French optical systems, and much progress has also been made over the last hundred years in the actual source of power. Girdleness lighthouse continues under the control of the Commissioners for Northern Lighthouses, and is a group flashing light giving two flashes every twenty seconds with a visibility of

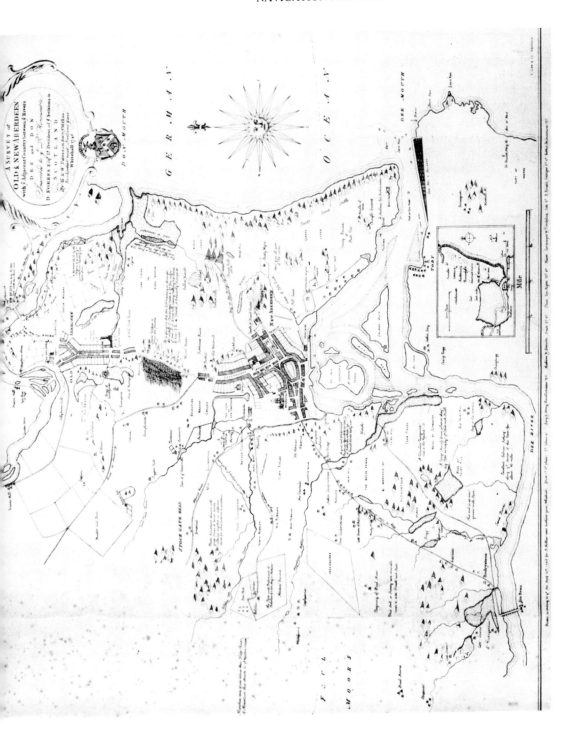

45   Survey of Old and New Aberdeen by G Paterson, 1746

twenty-two miles. The lighthouse is today also equipped with a Racon radar beacon. In the latter stages of nineteenth-century harbour construction, the Harbour Commissioners erected lighthouses at the extremity of the New South Breakwater and the North Pier. Today these continue in use. The new South Breakwater light characteristic is a red and green flash every three seconds visible 7.8 miles, and the North Pier shows an occulting white and red light which eclipses every six seconds and is visible nine miles. The North Pier is also equipped with a fog bell which is operated in conditions of poor visibility. All these harbour lights and the fog bell are connected direct to the Navigation Control Centre in the Round House where they are operated together with the navigation control lights.

Patterson's map of Aberdeen in 1746 shows many of the navigation facilities in the harbour, and depicts marker stakes on the sides of those areas of the harbour drying out at low tide. Soundings are, however, very sparse and opposite the Town Quay, a figure '12' appears which suggests that there was twelve feet of water—presumably at high tide. Patterson's map must have been considered unsatisfactory for navigational purposes since the magistrates subsequently commissioned the surveyor, Peter May, to undertake a detailed survey of the harbour and entrance thereof, together with the adjacent coast between the Rivers Dee and Don. From a navigational viewpoint, however, there is not much extra value in his map which gives little or no detail of the actual harbour itself. A large rock, known as 'Collsamon' appears just to the north of the Bar, and on the south side almost opposite the end of the bulwark is a beacon. Astonishingly, there is no beacon on the shoal immediately opposite the mouth of the harbour described by May as 'beach called Pointlaw under water at ordinary tides'. Whilst local shipmasters would know that on rounding the harbour entrance they had to head northwest close inshore by Pocra, a visiting shipmaster would not have this knowledge, and would face very real hazards if he strayed far from the channel. May's map shows a pier at Pocra at right angles to the channel, and the pierhead appears to reach relatively deep water which does not dry out. Along the south side of the inches appear to be a series of seven beacons marking the south side of the channel, but the approach to the Town Quay at the shore lands must have been extremely difficult, and the services of a pilot would be absolutely essential even for a local shipmaster. May states on his map that channels frequently shift.

The position had changed little when Smeaton undertook his surveys in 1769 and 1787. Judged by his drawings, there was an obvious variation in the

facing page
46   Map of Harbour area by Peter May, 1756

Scale of Scots Chains 24 E each

Road to the New Burgh

Don Bridge

Island

DON RIVER

High Water Mark

Arable Lands belonging to Mr Midleton

Sands & Bents

Sands & Bents

Sands & Bents

A PLAN
of the Coast and other
remarkable Places between the
Rivers
DEE and DON
Surveyed Anno 1756
by
Peter May

Old Brickwork

New Brickwork

Old Course of Don River

Tyle Brickwork

Sands under water at High Water

Bent Hillocks

Nether Lands

Road through the Links

KING'S LINKS

Gallow Hill

Broad Hill

GERMAN OCEAN

QUEEN'S LINKS

Ordinary High Water Mark

High White at spring Tides

Sandilands

Lands belonging to Aberdeen

ABERDEEN

Shoar Lands

New Arms

Gross overn

Footdee Kirk

Roper House

Carpenters Yd

Foundery

Pickerny

Willow Wervery

Low Water at spring Tides

BARR

Pinner Nunk

Mid Chingle Fishing

DEE RIVER

Rack Fishing

HAUGHS
of
TORRIE

Waellie Simmers

Beach under water at ordinary Tides

Point Law under Water at ordinary tides

Salt Pann

Beacon

Steep Banks

BAY OF NIGG

Old Town Kirk

References

AA. A Bulwork of Stones to keep the River Don in its proper Channel
BB. Lakes or Ponds of Water common-ly called Canno Sweets Potts
CC. March Stones lately placed from which a straight line extended is meant to divide the Coast Fishing between Dee & Don
D. A Big Stone lying on the north side of the Barr & appearing at low water referred to by the Witnesses it is called Collsamon
BARR is a Shoal in the River's Mouth made with the fluxion of the Tide & River which shifts almost in every storm
E. A place on the north side of the River's mouth commonly called the Haum or bed
F. The Channel for bringing in Ships to the Stone Peer
G. The stone Peer where the Ships lye at Anchor
HHHH See Bulwarks of Stones made to keep the Water in its proper channel
III The strokes mark't as on the margin are Stoops fixed for hauling out & in Ships to the Harbour
N.B. The Current of the water running deep-er on the sides than in the middle makes a jetting out at the mouth of the Dee which is commonly called the North & South Channels but these channels frequently shift

At Aberdeen the sixteenth day of June in the Year One thousand seven hundred and fifty six in presence of Sir James Reid of Barra Baronet one of His Majesty's Justices of the Peace for the County of Aberdeen

Compeared Peter May Land Surveyor who being solemnly sworn made oath that in obedience to the Magistrates of Aberdeen he made a true and faithful Survey of the Harbour & entry thereof with the adjacent Coast between the Rivers Dee & Don and that this Plan is a just and accurate description of the premises surveyed by him the deponent containing the whole bearings & distances as therein described together with the high and low Water Marks both at spring & Neep Tides all which is mark't locally on the Plan as they were the time of the survey which was taken the fourteenth day of June Current all which he declares to be truth as He shall answer to God Signed James Reid J.P. Pet May Surveyor

This is an exact Copy of the original but contract-ed to a smaller size which is likewise attested by the said Peter May

main channel thus confirming May's assertion that the channels frequently shifted. Smeaton showed limited evidence of beacons or other navigational aids.

The earliest existing recorded reference to any pilot service in Aberdeen is contained in the report of Philopoliteius in 1685. Clearly, however, pilots were guiding ships over the bar and through the tricky entrance channel long before this. One early pilot, Robert Lindsay, is said to have made a chart of the harbour—probably in the fifteenth century. These past pilots were subject to little regulation, they were unqualified, and appear to have offered their services on a competitive basis. The Harbour Act of 1773, however, conferred powers on the magistrates and City Council of Aberdeen to appoint pilots, and to regulate pilotage by byelaw. In the subsequent Act of 1810, the magistrates and City Council were empowered to conduct examinations and to investigate the skill and ability of pilots. Under this Act, pilots licences were to be issued initially, and thereafter on an annual basis, and for the privilege of holding this licence the pilots had to pay an initial fee of five shillings for their first licence, with an annual payment of two shillings and sixpence thereafter. The 1810 Act also laid down the rates and charges for pilotage.

A Royal Commission of 1836 recognised the national importance of consolidating the law related to pilotage, and a succession of legislation followed, commencing with the Merchant Shipping Act, 1854. In 1877 the Aberdeen Harbour Commissioners issued detailed regulations for the local pilots, and also for the Captain Pilot who was also the port's Harbour Master. The Captain Pilot determined the actual number of persons to be licensed as pilots, he took part in examining as to their skill and ability, and he otherwise regulated their employment. The fine for acting as a pilot without a licence was £20—a vast sum of money in those far off days. The Captain Pilot had to approve the size and rig of the pilot boats. The pilot boat crew was prescribed as consisting of no less than six, of whom four had to be able bodied men who were licensed, and two could be active young lads. The master, or chief pilot of each boat had to have his own name and the number of his boat painted on the side in large distinct characters. The master or chief pilot of each boat also had to maintain his own boat in constant readiness during tide hours which were considered to be at least three hours before high water, and otherwise as directed by the Captain Pilot. The pilots were not allowed to convey ships out of the harbour until the Captain Pilot was satisfied that the rates and duties had been paid to the satisfaction of the Collector of Harbour Dues. The pilots belonging to one boat were not allowed to take charge of more than one vessel during each tide except with the consent of the Captain Pilot, and there were severe penalties if pilots neglected the signal of any vessel requesting a pilot. Detailed regulations also applied as to the rota, and when required by the Captain Pilot they had to provide a boat and at least two men to take soundings in the Navigation Channel, the harbour, and the dock.

The Harbour Commissioners had been appointed the Pilotage Authority for the Aberdeen District under the 1894 Merchant Shipping Act, which attempted to place pilotage throughout the United Kingdom on a sound basis. The Pilotage Act, 1913 was, however a more comprehensive means of regulating pilotage, and in 1922 the Board of Trade confirmed new byelaws for the Aberdeen Pilotage District. These required that a candidate for a pilot's licence had to furnish proof that he had at least seven years experience as a seaman or fisherman, that he understood the handling and management of vessels, how to bring them to anchor, and how to moor and unmoor, and to get them underway and to give directions for their towage if required. They had to produce certificates as to their good service, character, and sober habits to the Pilotage Authority. They had to have sound hearing and sight and undergo an examination by two examiners appointed by the Authority. At a later date pilots in Aberdeen, as in most other ports, were required to have Masters Certificates of Competency, and this spelt the end of the old Footdee pilots. These men had expert knowledge of the shoaling waters and changing channels in the harbour, but were clearly without sufficient experience to handle large modern steamships—particularly turbine ships with poor stern power and slow response times.

In essence pilotage arrangements have little changed in the intervening years. Aberdeen pilots are ten in number, are all master mariners, and currently remain self-employed. Aberdeen Harbour Board is the Pilotage Authority, and under the old 1922 Pilotage Order, they have delegated powers for the appointment, licensing, discipline, and recruitment of pilots to a Pilotage Committee. This Sub-Committee of the Board currently comprises two appointees of the Harbour Board—the General Manager and the Harbour Master—a shipowner, and a representative of the pilots. Examinations for pilotage licences are carried out by the Harbour Master and a Pilot. Proposals have been made by government that throughout the British Isles pilots come more closely under the control of the port authorities who have responsibility for safe navigation, and in due course they would then lose their self-employment status and become a part of the port authority staff.

The pilots have a modern pilot cutter for conveying pilots out to approaching ships, and for picking up pilots from departing ships. This is based on a traditional fishing boat hull form with modern alloy super-structure and a powerful diesel engine. The boat is fully equipped with radar, echo sounder, and the most up-to-date equipment, but is limited to a maximum speed of around nine knots. Experiments had previously taken place with a glass fibre boat capable of much higher speed, but this boat was unable to cope with North Sea conditions in bad weather, and it was considered that speed should be sacrificed in the interest of having a pilot boat able to proceed into open water in all weather conditions in order to provide a twenty-four hour service. There is a reserve pilot boat also designed with a fishing boat hull form, and this is used when the regular boat is out of service for annual maintenance or for repairs.

Following the extensive harbour reconstruction works in the nineteenth century, the Commissioners established leading lights on the line of the centre of the navigation channel, and also during the nineteenth century an official was appointed as the Keeper of the Leading Lights with responsibility

47   Modern pilot cutter, 1985

for their lighting and maintenance—much on the lines of conventional lighthouse keepers. The introduction of electric lighting, however, rendered this post obsolete, and the leading lights continue in use today but are operated by electricity and are controlled centrally from the port's navigation control centre. The navigation control for the port is housed in an hexagonal building known as the 'Round House' located at the base of the North Pier. There is no evidence of this structure until after Telford's earliest maps which suggests that it was constructed around 1810. The building was subsequently modified in 1947 when an extension was built at first floor level. The whole of the first floor is now used by the duty pilots, and a tide gauge is located close by so that both pilots and navigation control officers can see the depth of tide and thus assess the depth of water in the channel and harbour. The Round House was heightened in 1966 and the uppermost floor now contains a sophisticated console which controls all navigation lights and signals in the harbour. There is VHF radio communication links to ships, pilots and tugs, as well as connection to the public telephone and the Harbour Board's own computer system and internal telephone system. Because of the importance of navigation control, an emergency diesel electric generator has been installed in case of failure of the public supply. In 1975 harbour surveillance radar was installed and with the increase in harbour traffic navigation control officers were engaged operating on a twenty-four hour basis. With some 11,000 ship arrivals a year, activity can be very intense at times, and rigid control must be effected in the interest of port safety. Originally traffic was controlled by day signals comprising black balls which were formerly lowered and hoisted by hand, but latterly by electric motors. At night lights replaced them. Now, however, a modern high intensity electric lighting system is used in much the same way as road traffic lights. This is supplemented by the VHF radio links with the ships.

With increasing traffic intensity, there were obvious disadvantages in vessels homing from all directions on the harbour entrance, and as a result it was decided to establish a fairway buoy some distance to the seaward of the harbour entrance. This buoy now acts as a focal point from whence traffic heads straight for the harbour entrance.

On 22 August 1827 Alexander Hall launched Aberdeen's first steam tug the *Paul Jones*. Captain Urquhart was the master, and this craft had forty horse power engines and replaced labourers on the piers who previously hauled vessels into the port entrance using capstans. Some of these early capstans remain on the south side of the harbour entrance channel and serve as a reminder of the difficulties encountered in bringing ships into harbour in those far off days. The second and third tugs were the *Dorothy* and the

Samson built in 1843–4 and they performed a similar valuable service to the *Paul Jones* which had been put to work immediately after launching. There are records of further tugs in operation in 1847, and in 1858 two tugs, the *Heather Bell* and the *Victory* were busily engaged in helping vessels into and out of the harbour. Over the succeeding years many other tugs have given valuable service in the harbour, and in 1958, the Harbour Commissioners took over the former Aberdeen Steam Tug Company Limited, and their fleet of four tugs. The present harbour tugs *Sea Griffon* and *Sea Trojan* were built in 1962 and have a bollard pull of 14 tons and a free running speed of 11¼ knots. Mainly used for towage in the harbour area, they have been used also for towage all along the coast of North East Scotland and for salvage work.

Over the centuries the Harbour Board themselves and their forebears have operated a variety of harbour craft. Telford first introduced a dredging machine, and various improvements on this were used in the first half of the nineteenth century. Later the Harbour Commissioners operated their own

48 Harbour Board tugs *Sea Trojan* and *Sea Griffon* bringing in *Nachiharu Maru* with a cargo of phosphate from Nauru.

fleet of dredging craft which eventually comprised a suction dredger, a grab dredger, and various hoppers. In due course these craft became obsolete, dredging methods had greatly improved, and modern technology rendered the craft employed by the Board wholly unsuited and uneconomic. After very careful deliberation, and with some sadness, the Board's craft were all sold off, and outside contractors were utilised employing much more sophisticated modern equipment.

In essence, dredging of the sand in the navigation channel has to be carried out by high-powered suction dredgers. It is normally sufficient to carry out a short campaign each year in spring and this is adequate to maintain the depth of water in the harbour approaches. In the enclosed part of the harbour, however, suction dredgers cannot get close enough to the quayside and are unable to cope with rock, clay, and with material dumped in the harbour such as unwanted trawl doors, fishing nets, and warps. So bad is the dumping of unwanted material in the part of the harbour used by the fishing industry, that the cost of dredging this area is invariably double that of any other part of the harbour. For this internal dredging work, grab dredgers are used, but when undertaking capital dredging—i.e. when dredging virgin

49　Grab dredger and hopper lying alongside Albert Quay, 1956

material for the first time adjacent to new quays—then it is necessary usually to use a bucket dredger or a back-hoe dredger. Some concern arose in the 1970s when the bucket dredger *Afrika* brought up an unexploded wartime bomb which necessitated calling in service experts to make it safe.

The Harbour Board themselves operate a launch which is used by the Harbour Master for general purposes, and this boat is equipped with light anti-pollution gear for dealing with small oil spills in the harbour. This boat is also used for harbour inspection, and from time to time conveys personnel out to large vessels lying in the bay when required. Small works cobles are used together with two sea salmon fishing cobles and two river salmon fishing cobles. Aberdeen Harbour Board also licenses self-employed boatmen who operate their own boats for the handling of ships moorings ropes, and their duty is to take these heavy mooring lines to the quayside where their colleagues attach them to the bollards.

Aberdeen was one of the first ports to operate a lifeboat, and the last to

50   Sailing lifeboat being towed to sea

retain a lifeboat in private ownership. The first boat, paid for by Alexander Baxter an Aberdeen merchant living in London, arrived by sea from Sunderland aboard the whaler *Neptune* in 1803. The first lifeboat shed was built around 1810. Initially the lifeboats were managed by the Shipmasters Society, but in 1810 the Captain Pilot, Captain Freeman, assumed superintendence of the boat on behalf of the magistrates.

The story of lifesaving and of the lifeboats is well documented by Dr J L Duthie in his book *To the Rescue!*, a story of lifesaving in Aberdeen from 1802–1924. Over these years there were stories of great bravery, but equally stories of conflict between crew and Harbour Commissioners. The early lifeboats were rowed or sailed, but by the mid-nineteen-twenties they were invariably towed out by harbour tugs! In 1925, the Commissioners finally conceded that the Royal National Lifeboat Institution was best fitted to operate the local lifeboat service, and the RNLI took over and have ever since provided first class motor lifeboats. The present lifeboat *BP Forties*, largely provided by funds generously donated by British Petroleum, is one of the finest lifeboats afloat, and has already given great service and thereby saved lives. The Harbour connection has continued, however. The Board provides all moorings, provides a substantial annual donation toward running costs, and the Board's Harbour Master, Captain Brian Atkinson, in his role as Captain Pilot is, like Captain Freeman in 1804, the Marine Secretary and Launching Authority.

Over the centuries the navigation channel has been progressively deepened and widened, and currently has a maximum designed width of 33.5 metres at its narrowest point, and a maximum designed depth at high water ordinary spring tides of 10.4 metres. A minimum depth of around 6 metres is generally maintained at all states of the tide thus allowing Aberdeen Harbour to operate right round the clock irrespective of tidal conditions. At spring tides there is a tidal range in Aberdeen of 3.7 metres, and this is reduced to 1.8 metres at neap tides.

The largest ship ever to enter Aberdeen Harbour is a title claimed by many, each using different criteria. The longest ever ship was the bulk cargo carrier *Saint Marcel* which had a length of 166.0 metres; the broadest ship was the cargo vessel *Alemannia* with a beam of 22.18 metres, and the deepest draft vessel was another cargo vessel, *Persenk*, which had a draft of 9.14 metres. As a general rule of thumb, it is safe to say that, depending upon length, beam, and draft, Aberdeen Harbour can handle ships of up to 18,000 tons deadweight carrying capacity or a little more. There are five deep water berths, and the majority of the other berths in the harbour are maintained so that there is at least a depth of 6 metres of water at the lowest tide of the year.

The modern harbour presents a very different appearance to mediaeval times, and in particular the changes wrought over the last 200 years have been quite remarkable. Aberdeen Harbour has few natural advantages, the River Dee is navigable for only a very short distance, and in its original state had a very shallow estuary. There is a litoral drift of sand to the south which tends to move towards the harbour mouth, and without artificial protection, the estuary is vulnerable to easterly winds.

It has been shown elsewhere in this book that there was, in the nineteenth century, determined opposition to much harbour development. Happily, however, wise counsel prevailed and the foundation of the modern port infrastructure was laid. This had been developed, especially in the ten years between 1973 and 1983, and Aberdeen now proudly possesses one of the finest harbours in Scotland. Deep water, a well protected entrance, the latest modern navigation aids, and highly professional navigation control and pilotage services, all combine to meet the needs of modern industry. Research is in hand to evaluate further development—this will maintain the position of Aberdeen and serve its industrial shipping requirements well in to the next century.

51   mv *St Marcel*—one of the largest vessels ever to enter Aberdeen Harbour

Shipbuilding and Marine Engineering

The fortunes of the shipbuilding industry in Aberdeen Harbour have varied very greatly over the centuries. At times shipbuilding has been non-existent, whilst at other times Aberdeen has been the biggest shipbuilding port in Scotland.

Little is known about when shipbuilding started. Successive Scottish kings expressed great concern that the nation as a whole built insufficient vessels. Efforts were made by Robert the Bruce to encourage native shipbuilding, but alas his efforts were doomed to failure. Some 300 years later, in 1619, King James VI again tried to encourage interest in shipbuilding, but his efforts were futile as were those of the Duke of York in 1687 when, as Kings Commissioner in Scotland, he too met with failure. For the most part, early ships were built in Danzig, or the Low Countries, and a few were built in England.

Boatbuilding in Aberdeen had been carried out from mediaeval times when lighters were built for carrying cargo unloaded from vessels lying off Torry in the 'Gawpuyl'. Before this, rudimentary fishing craft had been built, but these were insubstantial and rarely ventured far from the harbour. In the early years of the nineteenth century a seventeen foot boat could be built in Aberdeen for £7 and a twenty-five foot boat for £15. In 1848 for the sum of £65 a thirty-nine foot boat could be built and equipped ready for sea. Rigged with two lugsails such a boat could carry some twenty tons with a crew of five.

The earliest record of shipbuilding in Aberdeen, as opposed to boatbuilding, occurs at the beginning of the seventeeth century when in 1606 the Council granted a licence to Alexander Davidson, a carpenter from St Andrews, to build a ship in the Trinity Friars yard with wood floated down the Dee from the Forest of Drum. The ship was named *Bonacord* on 28 July 1609, and set sail on her first recorded voyage on 23 November of the same year. There is no further record of shipbuilding during the seventeenth century although one Alexander Cumming, a boatwright, is on record as building small craft for local use.

In 1741 there was apparently a small shipyard at Torry, operated by the

Gibbons family. Some twelve years later, Simon Halliday, operated a shipbuilding yard at the south end of Footdee Village where he set up business as a shipbuilder. Halliday continued until some time after 1767, and meantime in 1764 James Bruce and James Jaffray set up nearby along the northeast side of the road leading to the new quay at Pocra. Halliday was succeeded by Walter MacKail, and shipbuilding appears to have increased rapidly so that according to the statistics of navigation and commerce in 1798–9 some twenty vessels were built with a tonnage of 1,863. At this time Aberdeen built the largest number of ships of any port of Scotland.

The famous firm of Alexander Hall & Company was founded in 1790, and by 1801 shipbuilding output had been doubled with forty-two vessels (3,461 tons) being built—this compares with the output of Glasgow being eighteen ships (1,095 tons). Wars with France limited overall trade, and shipbuilding fell into a decline even after the final defeat of France in 1815. John Duffus & Co built Aberdeen's first steamer, *Queen of Scotland* in 1829 for the new

52   Old ship-building yard, *c*.1897

Aberdeen Steam Navigation Company. This was a paddle steamer with a wooden hull specially constructed for coastal trade to London, and in the succeeding eleven years was followed by four similar ships from the same firm.

John Vernon & Sons were associated with the first of Aberdeen's iron ships, the *John Garrow*, of 1,800 tons built and launched from the yard in 1837. About 1815, the firm of J Duthie Sons & Co was founded by William Duthie in conjunction with his own shipping line between London and Australia.

Alexander Hall & Co originally established their reputation as builders of wooden craft, and between 1811 and 1877 the firm built no less than 290 ships varying from 20 to 2,600 tons. In 1839 they built *Scottish Maid* the forerunner of the great clipper ships for which Aberdeen became justly famous. Clipper ships were so named after the *Clipper Bow* pioneered on the *Scottish Maid* to a local design. The first of the new vessels was the *Torrington* built in 1845 to the order of Jardine Mathieson & Co which successfully competed with American ships on the Chinese opium trade.

Another famous shipbuilding firm, Walter Hood & Co, was established in 1839, and until their demise in 1881, they shared with Alexander Hall the distinction of producing the majority of clipper ships which achieved for Aberdeen such great renown. Of these, undoubtedly the most famous was the *Thermopylae*, claimed by many to be the fastest sailing ship in the world, and a fierce rival of the Clyde-built *Cutty Sark* and *Taeping*.

Other famed Aberdeen built clippers included in 1850 the *Stornoway* and the *Chrysolite*, amongst the first of the fast tea clippers, and in 1852 the *Cairngorm* which was the first to give the American clippers real competition. None, however, could compare with *Thermopylae*, the pride of Aberdeen.

The glorious age of the clipper was short; the opening of the Suez Canal in 1869 effectively marked the end of the clipper era. The last to leave the slipway in Aberdeen was the *Caliph* launched in 1869, but even before the demise of the clipper, Aberdeen was already establishing a reputation for the building of steel ships and the production of marine engines. Hall Russell & Co, having purchased the premises of the Aberdeen Ironworks, commenced production of marine engines and boilers in 1864, and three years later expanded their business by building iron ships. Initially the company built only small coasters, but in the closing years of the century joined other builders such as Hall & Co and John Duthie Sons & Co, in the construction of steam trawlers and drifters. The first steam trawler to be built in Aberdeen, the *North Star*, was launched from Duthie's yard in 1883 and engined by Hall Russell & Co. From thenceforward, until 1902, no less than 267 steam trawlers were launched from Aberdeen yards.

Although shipbuilding continued up to the time of World War I, and throughout that war, there was a short boom after the war which was the precursor of a long period of depression. In 1925 Duthie & Co's yard closed down and the remaining three fought desperately to obtain new custom in order to remain in business. Activity increased during World War II as the Ministry of War Transport and the Admiralty made heavy demands on shipbuilders, with the result that a wide variety of craft were constructed varying from commercial vessels to a range of war-time craft which included frigates, corvettes, minesweepers, and even tank landing craft.

At the end of the war, shipbuilding continued at a high level of activity, for a short period, then rapidly declined. By 1963 there were only two effective shipbuilders in Aberdeen. In 1942 the share capital of Hall Russell & Co had been purchased by Burntisland Shipbuilding Co Ltd in Fife, and eleven years later they purchased the capital of Alexander Hall & Company although this retained its individual identity for some years. A very wide range of vessels was built after the end of the war, trawlers, freezer stern

53   Launch of mv *Sugar Producer* from Hall Russell's shipyard, 1957

54 Launch of mv *Sugar Transporter* from Hall Russell's shipyard, 1957

trawlers, chemical and oil tankers, car passenger ferries, and including ships of up to 7,100 tons. In 1965 Hall Russell built the first UK oil rig supply vessel. Three years later Burntisland went in to liquidation and Hall Russell, now owned by Northern Shipbuilding & Industrial Holdings Ltd had to write off £100,000 in unsecured loan stock and current account balances.

John Lewis & Sons Limited had been founded in 1917 at Torry, and their shipyard was extensively modernised immediately after the war. Vessels of up to 2,500 tons gross were built, but much of the construction was for the fishing industry. Sadly, the boom came to an end all too soon. After building some eighteen ships of 31,545 gross tons in 1959, by 1962 this had reduced to thirteen ships of 10,182 gross tons. In 1972 the Lewis shipyard was sold to the John Wood Group, and subsequently their shipbuilding activity virtually came to an end. The company still retains a shipbuilding capability, and maintains an important presence in Aberdeen in marine engineering and ship repair work. The former shipyard is now largely used in connection with offshore services and engineering. The company built a slipway on which vessels of up to 1,600 tons could be drawn out of the water for overhaul and repair, but this was infilled in 1985.

Under the terms of the Aircraft and Shipbuilding Act of 1977, the government nationalised the larger shipbuilding yards in Britain, and the famous Hall Russell yard came under the ownership of British shipbuilders. The company continued under state ownership actively building vessels of high quality and specialised design, but a change in government policy meant the yard was placed on the market and returned to private ownership, Aberdeen Shipbuilders Ltd. In recent years, the yard built a large number of offshore patrol vessels for the Royal Navy in addition to a number of tugs and naval salvage vessels. The company have a first class dry dock built in 1972 of 112.8 metres length, and in 1982 brought into use a covered shipbuilding way as part of a modernisation and re-equipment programme. The yard covers an area of 15.5 acres including workshops, and a fitting out quay of over 100 metres length. The quay is equipped with a crane of 72 tons capacity. Happily, the traditional shipbuilding skills live on in Aberdeen, and the port retains the highest reputation for quality of workmanship in both shipbuilding, marine engineering, and ship repairing.

Shiprepairing has always been a major service in Aberdeen, and the first graving dock was built on the site of the present day Atlantic Wharf in Albert Basin between 1882 and 1886. This dry dock was closed on 30 April 1913, but at the request of the Admiralty, it was re-opened in April 1914 until 10 December 1915 when it was finally closed. It was finally removed between 1924 and 1927. The first floating dry dock was installed in 1899. This early pontoon dock was purchased from Messrs Clark & Standfield at a cost of £8,057, and was built of iron. It gave good service, and was eventually replaced by the present pontoon dock No 1 built by John Lewis & Son in Aberdeen in 1953 at a cost of £78,315 including consultants fees. The second pontoon dock, No 2, was built in 1905 and replaced in 1967.

The largest pontoon dock, No 3, was built by Vickers, Sons & Maxim Ltd, Barrow-in-Furness in 1911. With a lifting capacity of 5,350 tons, and a length of 310 feet, this large floating dry dock was moored in a specially prepared berth at Pocra. By 1933 this large pontoon had handled some 4,612 ships with a gross tonnage of 1,089,072 tons. The largest vessel had a length of 400 feet and a deadweight of 5,400 tons. Eventually, however, it reached the end of its economic life and was sold in 1960.

In addition to the two remaining pontoon docks owned and operated by the Harbour Board, Hall Russell Limited built a new 113 metre graving dock in 1972, and more recently Wood & Davidson built a new slipway in the River Dee which was able to handle ships of up to 1,600 tons before

55 sv *Elissa*, the last surviving sailing ship built in Aberdeen. Now preserved at Galveston, Texas, USA

withdrawal from use. There are, therefore still extensive dry docking facilities, and several firms still carry on the traditional skills of ship repairing and marine engineering using the latest modern technology.

The last Aberdeen built sailing ship remaining afloat is the *Elissa*, now owned by the Galveston Historical Foundation in Texas, USA. This fine old vessel, built in 1877 for Henry Fowler of Liverpool, traded world-wide changing ownership many times. After lying as a hulk in Piraeus, Greece, the old ship was towed across the Atlantic to Galveston where she has been lovingly rebuilt and renovated—all to the original design. The old barque was rededicated on 4 July 1982, and in October 1984 a presentation ceremony was held on board at which many old plans of Aberdeen Harbour and original drawings, were handed over to the safe keeping of the Foundation by the writer. The ship is now well maintained, and her new owners preserve her as a monument to a bygone era, and as a lasting tribute to the great shipbuilders of Aberdeen whose skilled craft still continues to this day.

Table 6 Ships built in Aberdeen 1960–84

Year	No.	Tonnage		Year	No.	Tonnage	
1960–1	20	4,091	nrt	1974	3	1,159	nrt
1961–2	11	4,599	,,	1975	6	6,004	,,
1962–3	9	3,161	,,	1976	7	6,246	,,
1963–4	9	4,944	,,	1977	3	2,652	,,
1964–5	14	2,979	,,	1978	5	2,105	,,
1965–6	7	3,675	,,	1979	4	2,376	,,
1966–7	6	6,043	,,	1980	3	1,677	,,
1967–8	9	5,760	,,	1981	2	1,417	,,
1968–9	10	6,151	,,	1982	2	3,747	,,
1970	8	3,145	,,	1983	1	763	,,
1971	9	5,511	,,	1984	3	2,289	,,
1972	12	2,838	,,	1985	3	763	,,
1973	9	2,520	,,				

Harbour at War

In its very long history, Aberdeen Harbour has figured prominently in much war-like activity. The raids by the Vikings have already been mentioned, and it may very well have been that the Roman armies of Agricola were supported by sea before the battle of *Mons Graupius* in AD 74. It seems much more likely, however, that the harbour was used by Roman support vessels in AD 209 when the Emperor Severus carried out punitive raids against the Picts in the north.

A fortification stood on the Girdleness headland in times of old, and traditionally this has been associated with Wallace. It is alleged by some historians that Wallace destroyed the English ships in the harbour belonging to King Edward I in 1297, thus cutting off the means of retreat of the English garrison who had lodged in the castle after setting fire to the Town. The castle itself commanded a fine view of the harbour and the Dee estuary from its vantage point on Castle Hill, but little is known of this fortification save that it was repaired by Richard Cementarius, the first Provost of Aberdeen, in 1264.

It is known that piratic depredations took place off the harbour entrance, but there does not appear to be any record of pirates entering the harbour itself. Mentions of pirate attacks occur in 1273, 1302, 1365, and 1369. Clearly the citizens felt threatened, and a harbour boom was improvised and a block house or fort was erected on the north side of the harbour entrance in 1477. This was reported to be initially a square building 36 feet in length by 18 feet in width with 6 feet thick walls. In 1532 this fortification was replaced by a circular building with 6 feet wide walls and a flat roof with a watch house for the look-out. At around the same time a watch tower was erected on the Torry shore opposite, but by the middle of the seventeenth century, this had deteriorated to a ruinous condition. The blockhouse mounted a battery of ten cannon which were twelve pounders, and this gave protection covering the harbour entrance right up to the time of its demolition around 1781.

It would seem that the difficult nature of the entrance channel, and the problems in negotiating the bar provided a natural protection from invasion,

56   Site of old Blockhouse, Pocra

57   Entrance to Torry Battery

58   Torry Battery overlooking the Harbour entrance

and certainly the fortifications in the block house could withstand almost any seige from the sea, and would be capable of inflicting severe damage upon invading vessels which could in any event only negotiate the harbour bar at certain states of the tide.

In 1588 there were strong local fears of possible invasion by the Spanish Armada, and in fact the Armada is reported to have been seen in Aberdeen Bay. No landings were made, and in fact the Spanish vessel *Santa Catalina* struck the rocks at Collieston and sank close by. Shortly afterwards the harbour became the scene of great activity when a local vessel, the *St Nicholas* was fitted out and victualled at the expense of the town to form a part of a Royal Squadron required to convoy the bride of King James— Princess Anna of Denmark and Norway—to Scotland. The *St Nicholas* dressed overall left the harbour on 16 April 1590 under its temporary master who happened to be one of the magistrates. The vessel was essentially part of an armed force but there is no record of it having ever been in action.

Despite flourishing trade in the previous century, by 1656 Aberdeen only had nine locally owned vessels and much trade was carried out by Dutch ships. As a result, the Town Council were reluctant to obey a directive to seize Dutch shipping in the harbour when war broke out with Holland in 1665. Around this time there were often lively incidents in the harbour, and both Dutch and Spanish warships were frequently in Aberdeen Harbour together although at war with each other.

The harbour appears to have played little active part in the civil troubles of the Reformation, and of the early part of the seventeenth century, but was much affected by decline in trade. In the following century, however, it was used by ships engaged in the slave trade, and it is believed that this detestable trade resulted in over 600 people, many of them children being kidnapped and sold into slavery. Press gangs kept close watch on the streets of Aberdeen, especially in the harbour area, and suitable persons were attacked, captured, and forcibly taken aboard slave ships. It would appear that the slaves were transported at around 40 per time, and groups of potential slaves were imprisoned in a tenement on the green which was only destroyed in the early part of the present century. Most of these early slaves went to North America for working on the plantations.

Aberdeen Harbour had a part to play in events leading up to the defeat of Prince Charles Edward Stuart at the Battle of Culloden. In the spring of 1746 a government army arrived by sea at Aberdeen Harbour, and after disembarking, marched northeast to take their part in the short action on Drumossie Moor, Culloden, on a cold, wet day on 16 April 1746.

The Torry Battery, completed in 1860 toward the end of the Napoleonic wars was built with a view to protecting the harbour against invasion. By this time improvements had been made to the harbour which had thus become much less subject to the vagaries of wind and tide, and a real invasion risk was considered to exist. Following the Battle of Waterloo in 1815, Torry Battery became surplus to requirements long before it had been completed, and was fortunately never called upon to fulfil the function for which it was originally intended.

In World War I the harbour had a very important role to play. Less than a month after the declaration of war two Aberdeen trawlers, the *Crathie* and *T W Irvin*, together with three other vessels were blown up by mines off South Shields. On 29 August 1914, the hospital ship *Rohilla* landed forty-five invalid sailors in the harbour, including Prince Albert who was later to become King George VI. These sailors were sent to local hospitals and nursing homes. The black-out commenced on 25 September 1914, but in fact the harbour was never attacked from the air. Many ships were attacked off the Aberdeenshire coast, however, and in October 1914 forty-nine survivors of HMS *Hawke* were landed at the harbour after being torpedoed by a German U-boat. In May 1915, four trawlers were sunk off Aberdeen by U-boat, and in this attack four of the crew were killed and fourteen wounded. Later in the same month the *Chrysolite* was sunk by U-boat.

The first air raid rehearsal took place on 4 May 1916, and was presumably evidence of local concern as a result of the raids by several Zeppelins all along the East Coast two days earlier. In this instance a Zeppelin was believed to have set out for Invergordon where the fleet was located, and it began its landward course at Carnoustie proceeding north-westerly through Fifeshire, Perthshire, and Inverness-shire, but the crew appear to have been bewildered in the Aviemore region, and to have turned north-eastward into Aberdeenshire, dropping bombs on Craig Castle and in the neighbourhood of Insch and Old Rayne before proceeding out to sea again at Newburgh. Had the Zeppelin crossed the coast a little further south, there is little doubt that the harbour would have received some unwelcome attention. This Zeppelin, the L20, was wrecked at Stavanger the following day on 3 May 1916. The Armistice signed on 11 November 1918 marked an end to the war in which a vast number of Aberdeen vessels were lost with substantial casualties to their crews. The following day the black-out was lifted and the local community in the harbour began to return to normal. During the war years there had been a considerable fall in cargo handled in the harbour, and in 1918 fish landings had fallen to 15,219 tons compared with 117,753 tons in 1913—the last full year before the outbreak of war. Total exports and imports of goods showed a similar fall from 1,483,151 tons in 1913 to

254,542 tons in 1918. The tonnage of goods passing through the harbour did not achieve the 1913 level again until 1936.

Preparation for World War II began some three years before the actual outbreak of war in 1939. A Port Emergency Committee had been set up under the auspices of the government, and consideration was given to various aspects of harbour operation should war eventuate. On 3 August 1939 there was a reconnaissance flight by the renowned airship 'Graf Zeppelin', and this preceeded the outbreak of hostilities on 3 September. The 1939–45 war differed very much from the previous world war in that there was a continuous threat to the harbour, not just from seaward, but also from the air. Furthermore, the nation was threatened by invasion, and harbour activity took on a whole new aspect.

The first Aberdeen ship to fall a casualty of war occurred with the sinking of the local steamer s.s. *Rubislaw* on 28 November 1939, and shortly afterwards on 9 January 1940 a ship was bombed and sunk by German aircraft off Girdleness. Later in the same month, the *Ferryhill* of Aberdeen

59   HMS *Clyde* moored in Victoria Dock. Used for training of Naval Reserves.

was sunk, and on 7 March 1940 there was an air raid alert whilst a German warplane flew high over the harbour and city but no bombs were dropped. Eventually this aircraft was shot down by fighter planes from the fighter station at Dyce—now Aberdeen Airport. On 15 April 1940 a brigade left the harbour on the *St Sunniva* with other vessels bound for Norway, and in the summer of 1940 the first bombs were dropped on Aberdeen and a house in Tullos became the first casualty. Further raids followed in the same month, a school in Walker Road was burned, and in July the first really serious raid took place. In this particular raid, the harbour was an obvious target, but most bombs fell wide of the mark and the Neptune Bar close behind the Hall Russell shipyard was destroyed with over 100 casualties.

Further air raids took place on Aberdeen, and invariably the harbour was a prime target. Fifteen air raid shelters had been built in the harbour area, and provision was made to defend the port with anti-aircraft and machine guns. The principal anti-aircraft batteries were at Pocra and at the North Pier, the latter being equipped with a predictor. Machine gun emplacements were approved but never installed at Victoria Bridge, the North Pier, and the Pontoon Dock Jetty.

During the 1939–45 world war, Aberdeen Harbour became an important naval base, and the Admiralty had reserved berthage of around 4,350 feet out of a total then available of 19,299 feet. There was a training school for DEMS (Defensive Equipment, Merchant Shipping) ratings at Albert Quay which was equipped with davits, and from 1939 the RAF operated an air sea rescue unit at Torry adjoining the site of the present leading light—this was extended in 1943. Welfare facilities were not forgotten in the harbour area, and NAAFI occupied the first floor of the west end of Regent Shed from 1943 onwards. Fear of invasion was ever present before the Normandy landings, and there were road blocks at the North Pier and at the Old South Breakwater, both being located at the inshore ends. The harbour was surrounded by a fence, and ladders on the North Pier were immobilised with barbed wire entanglements. There were some six pill boxes in the harbour area, and nine mine observation posts in strategic locations.

A boom across the harbour entrance was operated by winches located on Abercrombies Jetty to the east of the Round House, and on the breakwater opposite. Provision was also made at the end of the South Breakwater for the installation of torpedo tubes. The new South Breakwater also had a searchlight. There was a separate harbour ARP (Air Raid Precautions) detachment with five posts and a report centre in Weigh-house Square. The ARP organisation was run quite separately from the Port Emergency Committee which, as previously mentioned, had been formed some three

60   Pill box guarding entrance to Harbour opposite Marischal Street, 1940–45

61   Barbed wire entanglements protecting the Harbour at Market Street, 1945

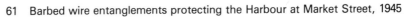

years before the war and carried on throughout the war until the cessation of hostilities.

In the course of the war there were 364 'Alerts' in the City of Aberdeen, many developing into full-scale air-raids. The harbour area was frequently hit, no less than forty-nine bombs dropping on the port. An interesting sequel occurred in the mid nineteen-seventies during major dredging operations when an unexploded bomb was discovered and subsequently disposed of by the military. It had been known from war time records that one unexploded bomb had been unaccounted for, and it was perhaps fortuitous that observant crew members of the dredger were able to detect the bomb and that it was safely removed—the consequences might easily have been tragic.

Bomb damage to Harbour Commissioners property amounted to £13,261 of which £9,017 was incurred in repairs at Albert Quay after the raid of 7 August 1942. In all, there were nineteen actual direct attacks on the Harbour itself with many near misses recorded. Perhaps the luckiest escape was when a bomb landed at the foot of Marischal Street at Regent Quay on 21 July 1941 narrowly missing an ammunition ship by a few yards. Had this bomb struck the ship, a vast area of the City centre as well as the harbour itself would have been completely devastated.

The Harbour was deemed sufficiently important to claim the attention of the German propoganda chief, Dr Goebbels. On at least two occasions, extensive damage to the harbour was claimed when not a single bomb had been dropped. On another occasion, 11 August 1941, enemy radio stated:

> Last night several German bombers attacked Scotland's most important eastern harbour—Aberdeen. Aberdeen is the chief harbour for the supply of foodstuffs for Scotland and also the principal base for trawlers and herring drifters. The raid was most successful. Several huge fires were observed by our bombers as they left for home. Great damage was done to the harbour installations.

On that particular occasion two bombs were dropped on the Bay of Nigg. One landed on the rocks and one in the sea!

As in World War I, World War II had a very detrimental effect on the traffic of the harbour. In the last full year before the commencement of hostilities, 1938, a total of 1,393,826 tons of goods passed through the harbour, and the ultimate low occurred in 1945 when only 795,261 tons were shipped. New plans for the harbour were prepared after the war, and within a very short time the harbour had returned to normal, and new improvements were under way.

62 Bomb crater in Marischal Street, July 1941

Royal Occasions

Although early Pictish Kings doubtless visited Aberdeen and utilised the Dee estuary for ships, the earliest Royal record is the grant in AD 1136 by King David I of a right for Nectan, the first Bishop of Aberdeen, to levy charges on vessels using the harbour.

As mentioned earlier, however, Royal attention could at times be less than friendly—as in the unwelcome visitation of the Norse King Eystein in the twelfth century; or it could be of a festive nature—as in the subsequent visit a few years later of the Viking leader Swein Asleifsson to join the Scottish king in an orgy of feasting and celebration. The festivities are recorded as having lasted over a month, and took place on a site believed to be approximately where the Harbour Office now stands. This marked the last of the warlike incursions of the Vikings, and thereafter a long tradition of peaceful trade has been maintained with Scandinavian countries which persists to the present day.

There can be little doubt that from the twelfth to the seventeenth century there were many royal visits to the city and harbour, both by Scottish kings and by visiting royalty—some of whom may well have been English kings in support of their armies. In 1319 King Robert I (The Bruce) granted a Charter to the City of Aberdeen in which he presented to the citizens the valuable salmon fishings of the Dee and Don, along with several square miles of Midstocket Forest. These fishings were the subject of several subsequent Royal Charters, and were in the fullness of time sold to private interests. Shortly before the turn of the century the Dee fishings were acquired by the Harbour Commissioners in order to permit the cutting of a new channel for the River Dee, and embark upon a scheme of harbour reconstruction which materially affected the former owners of the hereditary fishing rights. These fishings are still operated by the Harbour Board over 600 years after the original grant by King Robert.

In 1596 King James VI granted a charter to the Provost, Baillies, etc of Aberdeeen empowering them to raise charges on goods and shipping using the harbour in order that the city magistrates could embark upon a scheme of modernisation and reconstruction in the harbour. Records of further Royal interest from thence forward are sparse, although a number of charters granted to the city affected the harbour. King Charles II passed through Aberdeen in 1615, but from that date until 1848 no record exists of any Royal association with Aberdeen Harbour.

On 5 September 1848, HM Queen Victoria accompanied her husband, Prince Albert, together with their family, the Princess Royal, the Prince of Wales, and Prince Alfred, embarked upon the Royal Yacht *Victoria and Albert* at London bound for Aberdeen. This first *Victoria and Albert was a* wooden paddle steamer, and arrived somewhat unexpectedly off Aberdeen at about 8 a.m. on the morning of 7 September 1848. The arrival was

63 HM Queen Victoria with HRH Prince Albert and the Royal Family arriving at Aberdeen
     Harbour, 8 September 1848

premature and caused some confusion, but by about 2 p.m. the same day loyal addresses were presented by the Town Council and senators of Marischal College. Prince Albert subsequently received the Freedom of the City. The prince then went ashore, drove to Kings College, and later returned to the ship. The formal landing of the Royal Party took place at 8.30 a.m. on Friday 8 September after a salute had been fired, and the Royal visitors stepped on to the quay passing under a triumphal arch which had been built especially for the occasion. The Queen landed at Waterloo Quay opposite the foot of Church Street, and subsequently the triumphal procession drove along Waterloo Quay, up Marischal Street to Union Street, and thence to Balmoral Castle on Deeside where they arrived late in the afternoon.

Another important occasion was the laying of the foundation stone of the North Pier Extension by HRH Prince Alfred, Duke of Edinburgh on 5 September 1874. This important event was attended by much pomp and pageantry. The Duke travelled from Balmoral to Aberdeen, and the foundation stone was duly laid together with a glass jar containing documents and coins. The 3rd Aberdeenshire Artillery Volunteers fired a Royal Salute from Torry Battery, and the 1st and 2nd Battalions of the Aberdeenshire Rifle Volunteers, and the 1st Battalion of the Kincardineshire Rifle Volunteers were in attendance. A banquet was given in the Town and County Hall for the harbour workmen at which the Bon-Accord Brass Band was in attendance. The accounts for the various expenses are still preserved in the Harbour records, and make interesting reading when compared with modern costs. The total cost amounted to £374.10s.2d. which included £113.7s.0d. for the Banquet, £22.4s.0d. for wine, £14.13s.0d. for a silver trowel and a glass jar, £16 for flags, and £2.2s.0d. for coins deposited in the foundation stone. The cost of hiring a train from Ballater to Aberdeen and back for Prince Alfred amounted to £24.9s.5d., but the hire of horse drawn carriages locally was more than twice as expensive at £55.9s.6d.

In 1894 HRH The Princess of Wales (Princess Alexandra) arrived in the Harbour aboard the Royal Yacht *Osborne*. This was the last of the paddle wheel Royal Yachts built of wood, and with three masts and two funnels. The next Royal visit to the Harbour was on 29 August 1914 when HRH Prince Albert, later King George VI, was landed in the harbour from the hospital ship *Rohilla* together with forty-five wounded sailors. He was taken to a local nursing home where he underwent surgery for removal of his appendix.

Again, a long interval occurred between Royal visits, but the next was no quiet disembarkation, but provided one of the most spectacular Royal visits to Aberdeen of all time. The Royal Yacht was named *Victoria and Albert*,

ABERDEEN HARBOUR.

VISIT OF

H.R.H. THE DUKE OF EDINBURGH.

The Harbour Commissioners beg to suggest that, on SATURDAY next, the 5th current, the Vessels in the Harbour should, during the Day, be

DECORATED WITH THEIR FLAGS & ENSIGNS,

and, in the Evening,

SHOW THEIR SIGNAL LIGHTS.

JOHN ANGUS,

TOWN HOUSE,
ABERDEEN, 2nd September, 1874.

Clerk to the Commissioners.

64   Harbour Commissioner instructions to vessels for a Royal Visit, 1874
65   Admission Card for Royal Visit, 1874

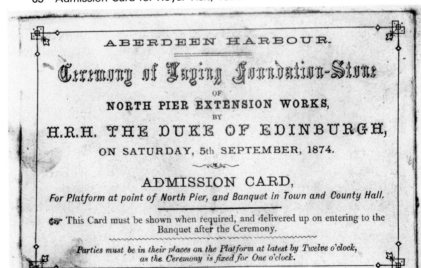

ABERDEEN HARBOUR.

Ceremony of Laying Foundation-Stone

OF

NORTH PIER EXTENSION WORKS,

BY

H.R.H. THE DUKE OF EDINBURGH,

ON SATURDAY, 5th SEPTEMBER, 1874.

ADMISSION CARD,

For Platform at point of North Pier, and Banquet in Town and County Hall.

☞ This Card must be shown when required, and delivered up on entering to the Banquet after the Ceremony.

Parties must be in their places on the Platform at latest by Twelve o'clock, as the Ceremony is fixed for One o'clock.

but this was in fact the third vessel to carry the name. The ship arrived off Gregness just before 2 p.m. on the afternoon of 4 August 1938. The arrival scene was described by the local newspaper, the *Evening Express*, as follows:

> It was an inspiring sight as the Yacht swept into Aberdeen Bay. Brilliant sunshine filled the Bay and patterned the sea with a myriad of dancing lights. Holiday makers on the beach stopped in their games and gambols to gaze across the waters at the magnificent ship with the Royal family on board. Several thousands were gathered along the promenade near the entrance to the harbour and on the piers. But the people who gained the best view of all were the hundreds who had the discrimination to choose Greyhope Road. They commanded a majestic vista from their high vantage ground looking down upon the whole scene and saw the arrival from the beginning to end.

After the Royal Yacht had anchored off the harbour entrance, the Harbour Master aboard the lifeboat delivered an address bearing the City's birthday greetings to the Queen. In due course the Royal barge was lowered and drawn up close to the foot of the gangway, and a few minutes later the King and Queen accompanied by HRH Princess Elizabeth and HRH Princess Margaret came down the gangway to the waiting Royal Barge to the accompaniment of blaring ships sirens. The Royal Barge came slowly past the breakwaters and into the harbour, and proceeded toward Matthews Quay where a floating landing stage had been specially constructed for the occasion.

> On Matthews Quay, garlanded and beflagged, and around the Royal enclosure, hundreds of people, many of them flourishing the Union Jacks, let loose a deafening roar of greeting, as the barge pulled in beside the punts and moored at the jetty to the south of the Dock Gates. Her Majesty looked up admiringly at the beautifully decorated awning, with its palms and shrubs and flowers, a lovely garden in the midst of the grimy docklands. (*Evening Express*, 4 Aug. 1938)

Over 600 yards of evergreen festoons had been used to decorate the enclosure, and over 2,000 pot plants had been borrowed from the links and parks department—so many as to require no less than eighteen lorries to transport them from the various parks!

The King stepped from the barge on to the pontoon and was received by the Harbour Master and Assistant Harbour Master before proceeding up the gangway after the Queen and followed by the two Princesses to be received by the Lord Provost, Baillies, Dean of Guild, and the Conveners of the four

Harbour Commissioners Committees. The Band of the Royal Scots Fusilliers played throughout before the Royal car left the harbour and passed huge crowds. The welcome followed the King and Queen and the two young Princesses all the way up Deeside to Balmoral for their annual holiday.

No Royal visits to the Harbour took place during World War II. Subsequently, in course of a scheme for effecting several post war improvements in the Harbour area, the Harbour Commissioners undertook the replacement of the old single track swing bridge between the north and south side of Victoria Dock, and on Wednesday 30 September 1953, HM Queen Elizabeth, the Queen Mother, carried out the formal opening of a new aluminium alloy double-leaf bascule bridge at the entrance to the dock.

66   HRH King George VI together with HM Queen Elizabeth, HRH Princess Elizabeth and
     HRH Princess Margaret, received by Harbour Master, Captain T A Wyness, after
     arriving in Aberdeen, 4 August 1938

A new Royal Yacht *Britannia* was built at Clydebank in 1953, and this vessel has been a regular visitor to Aberdeen Harbour ever since. The first visit was on 23 August 1954, when *Britannia* disembarked HRH Prince Philip, Duke of Edinburgh, after the world tour made by the Queen and Prince Philip that year. Regular calls in the Harbour were made over succeeding years with very few gaps. 15 August 1979 marked the eighteenth visit by the Royal Yacht to Aberdeen Harbour and, in fact, was the twenty-fifth anniversary of that first visit in 1954. To celebrate the long and friendly association between the officers and crews of Royal Yachts and the staff of Aberdeen Harbour Board, a presentation took place on 15 August 1979 at which an inscribed vellum was presented to the Flag Officer Commanding Royal Yachts, Rear Admiral Hugh Janion RN, and in return the Harbour Board was presented with a plaque bearing the crest of HM Yacht *Britannia*.

HM Queen Elizabeth visited the Harbour in 1977 to inspect the quay facilities operated by Seaforth Maritime Limited, and by happy coincidence these are immediately adjacent to the very spot where her great great grandmother first landed in 1848. This visit was made by Her Majesty and the Duke of Edinburgh whilst in Aberdeen as part of the Silver Jubilee celebrations.

On 3 July 1978, HRH Prince Philip, Duke of Edinburgh, made a private visit to the harbour in which he toured port facilities. Unfortunately, the weather could not have been worse for the occasion, and the Royal progress through the harbour was accompanied throughout by heavy rainfall. After an initial visit to the port's navigation control centre at the North Pier, His Royal Highness was subsequently taken on a tour of the harbour by the tug *Sea Trojan* and few visitors to the harbour have taken a keener professional interest than the sailor Prince.

More recently HRH The Prince of Wales was present in the harbour on 3 July 1980. The visit was part of a tour of the offshore survival training facilities provided by Robert Gordon's Institute of Technology, and the Prince saw demonstrations at sea and also in the harbour area where the college staff demonstrated various types of lifeboat and offshore survival capsules. The Prince took a very keen interest in the facilities, and in the equipment displayed on this unique specialised quay.

Another great Royal Occasion occurred on 5 August 1982 when HM Queen Elizabeth accompanied by HRH The Princess Anne visited the harbour, and opened the new fish market at Commercial Quay. Arriving in the Royal car, the Queen and Princess were escorted by the Chairman, George M Lawrence, and the author as General Manager. The Royal tour commenced with a display of harbour and fish market history followed by a display of fish and fish products. The Royal party then watched the salmon sales, saw fresh fish landed, and witnessed the daily auction of fresh fish. The formal opening ceremony then followed before an audience of invited guests mostly from the fishing industry. Afterwards, Her Majesty and Her Royal Highness inspected a nearby fish-house to see fish processing first hand. They then were shown over two Aberdeen fishing vessels before moving to the Harbour Office to sign the visitors book. Large crowds turned out, and the harbour took on an air of excitement and gaiety far removed from the day to day routine of a working harbour. Few Royal visits can have engendered such pleasure and such good will.

Calls in Aberdeen Harbour by Royal Yachts have changed somewhat over the years. At the time of the first visit by Queen Victoria in 1848, morning dress was the order of the day, and it is interesting to note that on this

67   HM Queen Elizabeth opening the new Fish Market, 1982

occasion Mr James Abernethy, the Harbour Engineer, carried a staff of office in his right hand as Chief of the Harbour Trustees Workmen. This staff of office or mace has not been seen for many years and its location is no longer known. It is probably now in some private collection. Even as recently as the early 1950s, morning dress was worn whenever the Royal Yacht arrived in the harbour, but the occasion is now very much more informal. When the Queen disembarks she is received by the Lord Provost, in his capacity as Lord Lieutenant of the County of Aberdeen, and the Queen and members of the Royal family are thereafter introduced to the reception party which usually comprises the Lady Provost, the Town Clerk in his capacity as

68   HM Queen Elizabeth, HRH The Princess of Wales, HRH Princess Ann and HRH Prince Andrew, received by Harbour Officials, August 1984

Clerk of the Lieutenancy, the Sheriff Principal, the Chief Constable, and the Chairman, General Manager, and Harbour Master of the Harbour Board. Normal lounge suits are now worn and the occasion is wholly informal with no pomp beyond the Marine guard at the foot of the gangway, and the officers and the yachtsmen of the Royal Yacht lining the ship's side.

Aberdeen Harbour is the only port equipped with a specially constructed royal brow—a gangway, steps, and platform—used to disembark the royal family irrespective of the height of tide. This, along with other specialised equipment for berthing the Royal Yacht, is kept in permanent readiness. H M Yacht *Britannia* has called at Aberdeen more often than at any other port except Portsmouth.

Standing at the entrance to the Royal River Dee, Aberdeen is the natural sea gateway for the private residence of the sovereign at Balmoral, which is in use for the Royal Family summer holidays each year. It is therefore not surprising that a very close liaison exists between the staff of the Harbour Board, the Royal Yacht, and other branches of the Royal Household. The Harbour Board and all their staff continue to take great pride in their long Royal associations which extend over 850 years.

69   HM Yacht Brittania

Salmon Fishings

One of the least known activities of Aberdeen Harbour Board is the exercise of the ancient heritable right to fish for salmon in the River Dee, and in the approaches to the harbour. It is believed that Aberdeen Harbour Board is probably the only port authority in the British Isles which carries on commercial fishing for salmon. Few activities generate such uninformed and often emotional commentary as salmon netting.

The rights to fish for salmon in Scotland—whether in the sea, in river estuaries, or in rivers themselves—belonged originally to the Crown. The heritable rights owned by Aberdeen Harbour Board originally stem from no less a person than King Robert the Bruce. On 10 December 1319 King Robert granted a Charter to his Burgesses and community of the Burgh of Aberdeen:

> . . . our foresaid Burgh of Aberdeen and our forest of the Stocket with the pertinence; to be held and had by the foresaid Burgesses and community, their heirs and successors, for ever, of us and our heirs in fee and heritage and in free burgage, by all their right meiths and marches, with mills, waters, fishings, petty customs, tolls . . .

This Charter effectively granted to the City of Aberdeen the right to fish for salmon in the Rivers Dee and Don, and it is under this act that the City acquired the forest of Midstocket and from which originated the City Common Good Fund. In a Charter by King James III in 1482, the Provost, Baillies, Councillors, and community of Aberdeen were freed for ever from customs upon salmon caught in the Rivers Dee and Don. Later, in 1551, Queen Mary permitted the Provost, Baillies, Councillors, and community of Aberdeen, and the majority of their fellow citizens to feu the fishings in the Dee and Don. This was followed by another Charter in 1553 granted by Queen Mary which permitted the granting to various persons the fishings of the Dee and Don. These rights were confirmed by King James VI and a Charter by King George III in 1804 granted the right of salmon fishing in the sea adjacent to the burgh lands in Kincardineshire.

Down the centuries, the heritable rights were subsequently sold or granted by the City to private individuals. Eventually by an Act of 1871, the Aberdeen Harbour Commissioners were authorised to purchase salmon fishings to facilitate harbour development, and were empowered to borrow money for the purpose.

Salmon fishings in general were regulated by several Acts passed by the Scottish Parliament up to 1705. Many subsequent statutes regulate the manner in which heritable rights have to be exercised—in particular the Salmon Fisheries (Scotland) Acts of 1862, 1868, and the Salmon and Fresh Water Fisheries (Protection) (Scotland) Act 1951. There is much other legislation and case-law regulating particular aspects of salmon fishing, and these laws are both complicated and protective. Few other commercial activities are governed by such rigid constraints—albeit that they are mainly designed to protect the fish and to ensure that the salmon species is not endangered.

Salmon is on record as being predominant amongst the earliest fish to be shipped out from the harbour. By 1789 as much as 1,890 barrels comprising 4 cwt each of Dee salmon were sent to London, and a somewhat lesser quantity of 1,667 barrels from the Don were sent to the same destination. Much of this was exported from London after salting. Salmon comprised a major part of the diet of the citizenry, and was often considered suitable only for servants and much too common to be consumed by their employers!

Each year mature Atlantic salmon return from their feeding grounds in the sea to spawn in the upper waters and tributaries of the River Dee. Fish returning to spawn after only one winter in the sea are known as grilse, and the remainder, which spend two or three winters in the sea or more, are known as salmon. Spawning in the upper reaches and tributaries of the river occurs from October to January, the eggs hatch in the spring into alevins which then develop into small salmon fry. After their first year of life the fry are known as parr, and during the spring of their second, third, or even fourth year they become smolts and descend to the sea during the summer to migrate to feeding grounds off the coast of Greenland and elsewhere in the North Atlantic. After spawning, the spent fish, now known as kelts, generally die, but a few do survive and eventually return to the sea. Sea trout are subject to like legislation and have a similar life cycle to that of the salmon, but they do not carry out such extensive long distance sea migrations.

Fishing seasons and fishing times are strictly controlled by law. Rod fishing on the River Dee commences on 1 February and finishes on 30 September each year. The time allowed for netting is somewhat less, and the law permits net operation from 11 February to 26 August. In addition to this limited fishing season, there is a weeky close time from 12 noon on Saturday until 6 a.m. the following Monday morning. During that period it is not permissible to operate nets, and all stake nets must have a clear opening or outlet, and all fly nets must be raised or lowered so as effectively to prevent the capture of salmon. Bag nets must also have their leaders removed. No net and coble fishing may be carried out at that time. Rods are only restricted on Sundays.

There are two net fishing methods in use on the Dee. A net and coble fishery is operated in the river, and this is the only method allowed within estuary limits. Originally the coble was laboriously propelled by oars, but in due course rowing cobles were replaced by motor cobles which similarly steam out into the river describing a circle, and return the end of the net to the beach where the other end is held by the fishermen. The two ends are then gathered together, and the net is drawn into the beach, any salmon caught are removed, and the whole process is repeated. It is illegal to operate fixed nets within river and estuary limits, and this type of net is therefore used in the waters of the sea either side of the harbour entrance. Known in law as fixed engines, these comprise bag nets which extend seawards from the shore suspended from floats and anchored in a fixed position. At the seaward end is a trap made of netting into which swimming fish are directed by a leader net. The purpose of the leader is to divert fish swimming parallel with the beach into the bag nets. Stake nets, or fly nets, are nets fixed to the foreshore by stakes, and these are a common sight along many Scottish beaches. The limits of the sea netting rights inherited by the Harbour Board under the 1871 Act commence to the northward from a line drawn through a march stone on the Broadhill close to the Beach Ballroom, and extend south to a line drawn opposite a march stone on the Girdleness headland.

The principal fishings acquired by the Board were the Raik and Stell fishings and the Midchingle fishings. These are shown on many old plans, and were operated mainly in the River Dee. Additionally, the proprietors of the Raik and Stell fishings owned the sea fishings to the north and south of the harbour entrance. Clearly it was not possible to develop the harbour whilst various individuals owned the right to fish in the waters, and in particular problems would have arisen when the River Dee was diverted into its present course in the latter part of the nineteenth century. Some £30,000 was paid by the Harbour Commissioners in compensation, and the Act of 1871 allowed the Commissioners to issue harbour bonds in order to raise monies with a view to compensating the former heritable owners.

An interesting map preserved in the Harbour Office shows the original boundaries of the fishings. The Midchingle fishings commenced a little above the Wellington Suspension Bridge, and terminated at a line drawn north north west from Torry Farm, and it would appear that there were originally three shots in regular use. Below this, the Raik and Stell fishings were mainly exercised in the channel of the river and on Torry Beach and inside the old South Breakwater. The Raik and Stell sea fishings commenced at the north boundary opposite the Broadhill, and stake nets were located all along the beach, and bag nets were anchored out in the Bay a little below the low water mark. The boundary between the River Dee and the sea as defined by the former Salmon Fisheries Commission describes an arc of about 1,000 feet from the head of the North Pier and the old South Breakwater. Bag nets, sometimes known as the horse nets, lay in the waters of the sea between this enclosed area and the new South Breakwater. The Greyhope fishings commenced from this point and continued round to a line drawn northeast from the Girdleness lighthouse. The Harbour Board also has rod fishing rights, and these are exercised above Victoria Bridge by the Aberdeen Angling Club.

At the time the former Harbour Commissioners purchased their fishings, there were some sixteen netting stations between Banchory, some eighteen miles up the River Dee, and the Bridge of Dee. Netting also took place in the tidal waters at the Pot and Fords fishings close by the present day Duthie Park in Aberdeen. The Dee Salmon Fishing Improvement Association was formed by the Marquis of Huntly in 1872 with the aim of improving the rod fishings on the Dee by leasing the net fishings below Banchory and removing the nets. Initially the cost was defrayed by proprietors with fishings west of Banchory, but in 1887 the charging arrangement was changed and based on assessed rentals on the fishings. Subsequently the Dee Salmon Fisheries Company Limited purchased the net fishings which had been rented by the Association, the company having been formed by members of the Association who subscribed the required capital in 1912. In 1914 they purchased the Pot and Fords fishings, and subsequently leased these on condition that they were only worked for twelve hours out of every twenty-four. In 1948, however, the company decided to take the fishing of the Pot and Fords into their own hands and worked them successfully for twenty years. The profits of the company were used to buy outright the netting rights of the lower proprietors with the result that the company has, with very few minor exceptions, now acquired all the netting rights between the old Bridge of Dee and Banchory. In the late 1960s the company were only working a forty hour week and with the general decline in the number of salmon entering the river it was decided that the fishings were an uneconomic proposition and the netting was stopped in 1968. The company still owns the right to operate nets, however, and is thus virtually the only party on the Dee other than the Harbour Board to own the heritable right to catch salmon with nets.

In an effort to help sustain the salmon species in the River Dee, Aberdeen Harbour Board have themselves made many voluntary reductions in the fishing time. In 1963 the weekly close time was increased from forty-two to forty-eight hours, and in 1970 with the conversion from tide working to shift working, one boat and crew were withdrawn from the river for twelve hours daily. In 1971 the annual close time was increased by two weeks, and in recent years that period has been further increased. The Harbour Board have also been substantial benefactors to the Dee District Salmon Fishery Board. Dee netsmen, including the Harbour Board, were responsible for the whole of the funding of the District Board hatchery at Dinnet on Deeside, and subsequently, the Harbour Boad paid for the radio equipment used by the Dee District Board Inspectors, and each year they are the largest single

70   Sweep netting for salmon in the River Dee, *c*.1900

contributor to the revenue of the Dee District Board. Contributions by way
of annual assessment in 1985 amounted to £30,868.

The Dee Hatchery at Dinnet has performed sterling service since becoming
operational. Each year live wild fish are caught in the autumn, they are
stripped of the male milt and the female ova and returned to the river. The
milt and ova are mixed together, and the fertilised eggs kept under controlled
conditions in fresh running water through the winter. When the eggs
develop, they are planted out in various burns and tributaries of the Dee
system, and they then hatch out along with eggs laid naturally in the normal
way. Cynics sometimes argue that some of these fish may not return to their
home river, but the proportions are likely to be identical both for eggs
planted by the River Inspectors and those eggs laid naturally. There can be
little doubt that the net-funded hatchery makes a major contribution to the
large numbers of Dee-born smolt migrating to the sea.

71   Sea salmon fishing cobble under construction, 1955

Most of the salmon caught in the harbour nets are sold by auction in the Fish Market. Promptly at 9 a.m. each day during the season, the Harbour salesman proceeds to auction part of the daily catch which mostly goes to merchants specialising in salmon and sea trout. Many of the larger fish go for smoking locally, but a large portion finds its way to Billingsgate and to the hotel trade. Nowadays the fresh wild salmon has to compete with salmon bred in fish farms, and prices are consequently much depressed. The farmed salmon can be placed on the market irrespective of season, they can be produced to a size preferred by the market, and after lying on a fishmonger's slab for a day or two, the quality and flavour advantage of the wild salmon over farmed salmon can no longer be discerned.

Over the years, harbour salmon fishings have attracted much unwanted attention. It is perhaps a natural instinct for the rod fisherman to blame the nets when catches are poor, and many have been the attempts to restrict netting activity. Anglers and owners of rod fishings have been known to maintain a long watching vigil in the hope of catching an unwary net fisherman in some minor breach of law—the flash of binocular lens in the sunlight has often revealed the watcher hidden in buildings, in telephone boxes, or in cars. Few of those determined to stop the net fishing have paused to reflect upon the consequences of stopping a practice which has continued without detriment to salmon stocks for over 600 years. If deprived of a large part of its revenue the Dee District Board would be forced to increase the assessment upon rod fishings, or would have to close down the hatchery and reduce the number of river inspectors and bailiffs—the choice is not a happy one.

From time to time it has been argued by one or two Dee rod fishermen that harbour traffic is affecting salmon fishing. The Harbour Board consequently have been subjected to complaints on the grounds that the activity of dredgers and an increase in shipping movements, were having a bad effect on salmon movement. It was argued in error that ships 'with propellers at both ends' caused so much vibration in the river that even Victoria Bridge was felt to vibrate! This was clearly untrue, and whilst some ships do have transverse bow-thrust propellers, the effect is really minimal, and usage is extremely brief. In past years, the Harbour Board had a dredger operating through-out the year, but now dredging is carried out in two very short campaigns so that the effect of dredging is now greatly reduced. With regard to numbers of vessels, the record post-war number of vessels using the port in 1956–7 was 16,696 when salmon catches were excellent for both rods and nets. Most of these vessels were small, and had propellers turning at the shallower depths where salmon swim, whereas large modern vessels have propellers much deeper down in the water, and thus any effect on salmon must consequently be much less today. The total number of vessels arriving in the port has now fallen to around 11,000. Modern ships are larger, their propellers turn at much greater depths with least effect on salmon—nevertheless catches by nets are now less than half those of 1956–7.

It has also been said in error that the Dee has become the 'Mersey of Scotland', and oil pollution has become a deterrent to salmon entering the river from the sea. That limited oil pollution has occurred from time to time is sadly as true in Aberdeen as in any other major harbour, although fortunately the scale locally is very much less. Oil, however, floats on water, at worst it is only a few microns thick, and since salmon rarely swim closer than within six inches of the surface, oil can hardly be a deterrent. Aberdeen is in fact one of the cleanest of Britain's major harbours, shoals of herring and other fish would otherwise not have ventured into the enclosed docks had the waters of the river and harbour been badly polluted.

In recent years, the stocks of salmon on both sides of the Atlantic have come under threat from many new influences. Firstly, about 1960, with the advent of monofilament nets, it became attractive to certain vessels which formerly pursued white fish to drift net for salmon in the sea areas off the Scottish coast. This was effected by laying long lengths of fine net across the migratory routes of the salmon returning to their native rivers. Such fishing was then perfectly legal, being outwith the scope of the prevailing salmon legislation, and it was also subject to no control. This offshore Scottish drift net catch, according to figures reported in Hansard, amounted to 9,000 salmon in 1960, 28,000 in 1961, and 115,000 in 1962. In September 1962 this type of fishing was made illegal around Scottish coasts but the long-term effect on salmon stocks caused by the huge hauls cannot be estimated. Secondly, in 1964–5 a new and very virulent disease, ulcerated dermal necrosis or UDN, appeared in Ireland and quickly spread to most Scottish rivers. In the Dee alone, the death rate rose from a normal 1,500 or so fish to 7,955 in 1967, 6,729 in 1968, and 4,465 in 1969. The disease is still in existence but the effect is now much less.

The greatest threat to the stocks of Atlantic salmon still arises from netting at sea. Firstly, there is netting legally carried on south of the border, and illegally north of the border. Secondly, there is large scale uncontrolled drift netting and long-lining for salmon in the International and inshore waters off Greenland, in the high-seas near the Lofoten Islands, and off the coast of the Faroe Islands, and, as mentioned, off the Northumbrian coast where English law does not pose the rigorous constraints of Scots law.

Critics of salmon netting often forget that, unlike the rod fisherman, the netsman is entirely dependent upon a strong and effective conservation policy for his livelihood, and for the commercial success of his venture. Aberdeen Harbour Board have consistently sought to trace and combat sources of pollution, substantial sums of money have been given to salmon-related scientific research projects, and much staff time and effort has been

72 Modern Salmon fishing

devoted to a wide range of scientific research and fishery management projects. If it were left to natural predators, disease, and anglers to control fish population, rivers left to their own would soon become overstocked with consequent increases in disease and mortality, and culling would become necessary. Sadly, outside agencies currently ensure that the Dee and all other Scottish salmon rivers are not left to establish a natural regime—seals, English drift netting, and heavy catches on feeding grounds off Greenland and the Faroes are taking such toll that overall stocks of the salmonid species are now in decline.

Just as individual riparian fishing owners do not publicise the catch for each private beat, so netsmen throughout Scotland do not publicise their individual catches except insofar as they are by law required to provide the information privately to the government. According to statistics published by the Department of Agriculture and Fisheries for Scotland, in 1972 only twelve per cent of the total Scottish catch of salmon and grilse was caught by rod fishermen. By 1982 the rod catch had increased to twenty-two per cent of the total nationally. In the Dee, however, the rods have in recent years generally caught a higher proportion of the salmon and grilse than the national average.

Initially the Harbour salmon fishings were purchased with some reluctance, and they have never been regarded as a significant money spinning source of Harbour revenue. In 1872 revenue from salmon fishings exceeded working expenses by £2,449.11s. 6d. and for the next forty or fifty years they continued to achieve modest profits. Occasionally, in bad years, a financial loss was sustained but sadly this has now become a regular feature, and in recent years the Harbour Board has suffered a continuing heavy financial loss on its fishings. There have always been substantial annual variations in catches of salmon, grilse, and sea trout, and often these follow a cyclical pattern. In recent years, however, there has been a downturn overall, and with the advent of huge quantities of farmed salmon upon the market, prices have not increased to offset the losses. It may very well be that in the near future Aberdeen Harbour Board will have to suspend or stop for ever the last of their salmon fishings. This would indeed be sad since the fishings have operated continuously for over 600 years, and they form a fascinating and interesting part of the history both of the city and of the harbour.

Trade Development

By the end of the eighteenth century, the harbour was handling some seventy-three inward cargoes and 248 outward cargoes annually. Cargo was moving to and from some fourteen different overseas countries, but the larger part of the trade was coastwise around the UK. The Treaty of Union had opened up trade to and from English ports, but trade with the Low Countries declined as local merchants searched for new markets.

Improvements to the harbour, a general increase in the size of ships, and the advent of the steamship all combined to greatly revitalise the trade of the port. Local industry expanded rapidly as new markets became more accessible, and the development of the Aberdeen granite industry is a typical example. In the eighteenth century granite exports were insignificant, the great Rubislaw Quarry having only been opened in 1775. By 1817 some 22,167 tons of granite were shipped in one year to London alone, and five years later this had increased to 34,687 tons. With newly improved harbour facilities and improved access, ships were now able to take local granite to destinations world-wide. A similar pattern developed for many local industries.

At the beginning of the nineteenth century there were no steamships using Aberdeen: the first steamship service to Aberdeen commenced in 1821, and by 1855 there were sixteen steamers based in Aberdeen, and by 1900 the number had grown to eighty-three. The Aberdeen Almanac of 1840 sheds much light on the regular harbour traffic of the day. Five local shipping lines are listed. The Aberdeen Steam Navigation Company owned four steamers engaged on regular services to and from London and Hull. A steamer left Aberdeen and London simultaneously every Saturday, and during the summer months every Wednesday and Saturday. On the Hull service, a steamer left Aberdeen on Wednesday and Hull on Saturday in the summer, but the winter voyage was only at ten day intervals. Occasionally a sailing vessel supplemented this service.

The Aberdeen, Leith, and Clyde Shipping Company had three steamships in 1840. Ships sailed to Leith every Tuesday, Wednesday, Thursday, and Saturday. Every Friday there was a sailing to Wick, Orkney and Shetland,

73 ss *St Giles* leaving Aberdeen for Shetland and Orkney

and on Tuesdays there was a sailing to Cromarty, Invergordon, and Inverness. The company operated seven smacks in addition to the steamers, and they operated a packet to Rotterdam every 6 weeks. Other companies served Newcastle, Dundee, and Burghead. The Aberdeen Directory of 1855–6 tells us that the fare for passengers sailing from Aberdeen to Newcastle on the steamship *Victoria* was 15*s*. 0*d*. in a cabin with steward, service and food included, and 10*s*. 0*d*. in steerage. The same ship also carried passengers from Aberdeen to Peterhead for 3*s*. 6*d*. cabin, and 2*s*. 6*d*. steerage.

By the end of the nineteenth century local shipping companies had increased in number. The Aberdeen Steam Navigation Company had six steamers engaged in the London trade, and the Aberdeen Newcastle and Hull Company had four steamers serving Aberdeen, Newcastle, Hull, Middlesbrough, and Stockton. The Aberdeen, Leith, and Moray Steam Shipping Company operated three ships to Leith, Invergordon, Inverness, Cromarty, Buckie, Burghead, and Lossiemouth. The Granite City Steam Ship

Company Limited operated a regular line to Hamburg and Rotterdam. The North of Scotland & Orkney & Shetland Steam Navigation Company Limited, with a fleet of ten, served Leith, Wick, Thurso, Kirkwall, Lerwick, Stromness, Scalloway, and Stornoway. Additionally James Crombie was the local agent for steamers serving Manchester, Liverpol, Stornoway, Stromness, Aberdeen, Dundee and Leith.

There were, of course, many other local Aberdeen shipowners, and the port was a regular port of call for a great many other British and Foreign shipowners. The shipping registered in Aberdeen increased from 199 vessels of 14,571 tons in 1795 to 368 vessels of 36,471 tons in 1804. By 1832 there were regular sailings to Quebec, Montreal, Picton, and Miramichi in Canada, and ten years later there were 224 vessels of 41,620 tons registered in the port. By 1857 there was a similar number of vessels registered in Aberdeen, but their tonnage had now increased to 65,000 tons—with the largest ship being 1,274 tons. In Scotland in 1857 only Dundee and Inverness exceeded Aberdeen in the number of ships registered (304 and 248), but all these were much smaller craft totalling only 59,000 tons and 11,673 tons respectively of which the largest ships were only 895 and 293 tons. The Aberdeen fleet included six whalers and six vessels in the Canadian trade.

74 Unloading a cargo of timber, *c.*1900

Much of the coastwise shipping from Aberdeen comprised cargo destined for transhipment to overseas ports not directly served from Aberdeen Harbour. It would appear that individual shipments were relatively small, and were for such variety of destinations that there was often not sufficient cargo to justify shipping direct overseas from Aberdeen. The same happened in reverse, and it is reported that Aberdeen imported over one million pounds of tobacco between 1873 and 1877—all delivered to Aberdeen Harbour coastwise by vessels sailing from English ports.

The nineteenth century saw the emergence of many important Aberdeen shipowners. The famous Aberdeen White Star Line of Messrs George Thompson & Co was renowned in the Australian trades, and Messrs I T Rennie & Sons also operated ships in distant trades. John Cook despatched his first ship, the barque *Carleton* to Quebec in 1848, and he then went on to develop trade to Scandinavia. Cook owned both steamships and sailing vessels, he engaged in the emigrant trades to Australia and New Zealand, and his ships were also employed in the tramping of general cargo. It was only in the twentieth century that the company ceased shipowning. The name continues, however, John Cook & Son Limited are to-day shipbrokers, shipping and forwarding agents, and stevedores in Aberdeen.

In the nineteenth century, imports consisted mainly of wheat, oats, flour, animal feeding stuff, manure, salt, chemicals, timber, iron, esparto grass, and of course fish. Exports were much less in quantity, and comprised oats, oatmeal, hides, beef, salt herring, soap, candles, granite, paper, flax, woollen goods, and miscellaneous manufactured goods.

The coal trade achieved great importance toward the end of the nineteenth century. Initially most firms started off by chartering ships, but companies such as J & A Davidson, Ellis & McHardy, George Elsmie & Co, and the Aberdeen Lime Company Limited all bought steamers for import of coal to the fast developing harbour. The emergence of the steamship with a heavy demand for coal bunkers coincided with the advent of coal-fired steam trawlers to generate a very substantial ship bunkering business in Aberdeen. Domestic and Industrial consumption also increased, and by 1891 some 416,946 tons of coal was imported annually, and by 1911 this had grown to 638,813 tons. The replacement of coal by oil as a fuel, and a change from sea to rail transport resulted in a sharp decline so that this commodity had disappeared from the Harbour almost completely by the early 1980s. A hundred years ago, the primitive and laborious method of unloading a coal cargo with iron buckets and tubs needed some seventy men. The occasional modern collier using high efficiency grabs on modern cranes needs less than ten per cent of the labour, and speed of working is more than quadrupled!

75   Unloading coal from ss *Spray*, *c*.1900

Agricultural produce was, and still remains, of vital importance to the trade of Aberdeen Harbour. We are told that in the twenty years to 1849 no less than 150,000 cattle (then valued at £3 million) were exported from Aberdeen. In 1849 some 7,800 head of cattle and 687 tons of meat were shipped—mostly coastwise. The advent of railways resulted in a decline in cattle shipments, but there was a resurgence toward the end of the century. With a new quay and a sale ring provided in 1886 and 1890 respectively at Pocra, the Canadian cattle trade greatly increased. At the turn of the century livestock traffic was still much to the fore as shown below:

Table 7   Livestock Shipments 1902

	Import	Export
Cattle	10,026	3,919
Pigs	2,606	2,875
Sheep, lambs and goats	26,873	—

By 1882, increased trade facilitated by harbour improvement had resulted in cargo throughput increasing to 690,068 tons. The magic million ton per annum mark was passed in 1895, and apart from two short, but largely wartime, periods 1915–23 and 1941–6, the traffic of the port has never fallen below a million tons per year. A record of 1,483,151 tons established in 1913 was not exceeded until 1968–9. In 1892 imports still predominated in a ratio of 3 to 1 over exports.

By 1901 the proportion of import traffic had increased further. Coal predominated, accounting for almost half the tonnage. Timber, white fish, and herring followed. Additionally barley, maize, flour, sugar, esparto grass, granite, bones and bone meal, salt, cement, woodpulp, iron, ale, and oilcake were all imported in significant quantities. Exports were dominated by granite shipments of which the majority were carriageway stones. Oats, oatmeal, oat husks, paper, preserved provisions and salted herring were, however, also shipped out in quantity.

Between the two World Wars, the pattern of trade in the twentieth century changed but little. The tonnage of fish landed was second only to coal, and imports of woodpulp had greatly increased as had flour, esparto grass, and mineral phosphates. Most significant, however, was the steady increase in import of fuel oils, paraffin, and petroleum spirit thus reflecting change from coal to oil fuel. Exports were still relatively small in volume, but again the pattern was showing signs of change. No longer did granite exports dominate, after coal bunkers, manufactured goods ranked second, with substantial exports of newsprint, paper, oats, herring, and salted fish.

At this time the London trade was still being carried on by the Aberdeen Steam Navigation Company Limited whose s.s. *Lochnagar* still holds many happy memories for older Aberdonians who well remember the excellent passenger facilities and catering. The North of Scotland & Orkney & Shetland Steam Navigation Company operated regular sailings to Caithness, Orkney and Shetland in their fine 'yacht-like' vessels. In 1933, the Harbour Guide books show a continuing regular coastal trade to and from Moray Firth ports, Dundee, Kirkcaldy, Leith, Middlesborough, Newcastle, Hull, London, Southampton, Falmouth, Plymouth, Bristol, Swansea, Cardiff, Liverpool, Manchester, and Belfast. The trade was, however, much reduced consequent upon fierce competition with the railways, and later by competition with road transport.

Most of the overseas trade was carried in tramp ships, few of which were owned in Aberdeen. There were also regular sailings to and from Hamburg, Bremen, Rotterdam, Antwerp, Gothenburg, Boston, and New York. The larger part of the exports were, shipped to other ports for transhipment, however, and in 1937 for example, less than one-third of the shipping using the harbour was engaged in the deep-sea trades. It is a sad reflection that Aberdeen shipowners, having dominated the trade of the nineteenth century had, by the twentieth century, ceased to be of any real commercial significance except for fishing and offshore support vessels.

War interfered with the trade of the harbour twice during the twentieth century. During these periods munitions and military traffic assumed considerable proportions, and inevitably the traditional trades, including fishing, fell into decline. In 1945 total tonnage had fallen to only 795,261 tons with coal still the largest single commodity at 300,062 tons, but significantly, imported oils at 72,427 tons now represented almost ten per cent of total traffic. Exports in the immediate post-war era comprised largely manufactured goods, oats and oatmeal, and potatoes.

Following the return to peace time trading, the traffic through Aberdeen Harbour was resumed initially on a similar pattern to that preceding the war, but change was imminent. Imports soon began to increase, and the trend

76   mv *Hannover* carrying a cargo of containers and general cargo from, Houston, USA to Aberdeen

continued steadily upwards. Exports, however, faltered from 1960 to 1970, but have increased steadily ever since. Three very important factors affected post-war shipping. Firstly, greatly improved road and rail communication spelled doom for the larger part of the coastwise regular traders, and apart from the services to the northern isles, none has survived on a regular basis. Secondly, the increase in ship size in order to attain greater economy of operation produced pressures to reduce the number of ports of call—especially in the ocean trades. Finally, and most important of all, the high cost of cargo handling, and the need to expedite ship turn-round and reduce time in port has led to a revolution in cargo handling methods. This has resulted in the evolution of new unit-load cargo handling techniques, and in turn cellular container ships and ro-ro (roll-on, roll-off) ferries based on ports in the south have effectively syphoned much traffic away from all the major ports on the east coast of Scotland.

The National Dock Labour Scheme, introduced initially during the war and continued ever since, has also resulted in some traffic deserting the larger British ports in favour of small ports. In Aberdeen, it has been estimated that up to half a million tonnes of cargo has been lost to smaller ports to the north and south which are outwith the national scheme. In Aberdeen, as in

77 Modern ferry, mv *St Clair* operating a regular passenger and freight service between Aberdeen and Shetland

Dundee, the Forth Ports, Glasgow, and almost all other major British ports, dockers are subject to rigid and inflexible legislation. They are, very properly, paid a regular salary irrespective of the vagaries of trade, they are thoroughly trained in modern handling techniques, and they have the benefit of a pension scheme. Few of the non-scheme ports have similar benefits, mostly men are employed on a casual hire and fire basis, they are untrained, have no pension provided, and are not paid if there is no work. Clearly stevedoring costs are very much less in these ports, and although speed of working is generally much slower, manning scales and working times are often more elastic. Every major scheme port in Britain has thus been undercut in terms of stevedoring costs, and Aberdeen has been a victim of this unfair competition just as has Dundee, Forth, Clyde, and almost every other major British port.

By 1956, apart from the Northern Isles services, the only regular coastwise service was operated by Coast Lines to London (weekly), Liverpool, Belfast, and the Outer Hebrides. Now only the services to Shetland and Orkney survive, and since 1978 these services have been modernised with new drive

78   Loading passengers' cars, P & O Ferry mv *St Clair*

on-drive off facilities, a new passenger lounge, new warehouses and animal lairages. The service, operated by P & O Ferries, successors of the North of Scotland and Orkney and Shetland Shipping Company, use two modern vessels. The mv *St Clair* is a passenger and freight ferry sailing three times a week on Mondays, Wednesdays, and Fridays at 6 p.m., and mv *St Magnus* sails up to three times per week with freight only.

In 1960 the surviving short sea and ocean trades comprised regular liner services to Netherlands, Norway, Sweden, Finland, and to Canada and USA. The latter service, however, soon fell victim to the container revolution, and cargo moved to services operating from the Clyde and from English ports. The services to Netherlands and Norway remain, but are in the hands of new operators.

By far the greatest development in post-war trade resulted from the discovery of oil deep in the earth beneath the waters of the North Sea. The history of this new traffic is fully dealt with elsewhere, but the nature of the cargo is worthy of special comment—especially as half of the Harbour revenue on ships and goods derives from offshore installation traffic. Every hole drilled in the search for, and in the production of, oil necessitates the use of drilling mud, steel casing and cement. The oil rigs or platforms require

79   mv *Stena Germanica* used for carrying personnel to and from Oil Rigs

80   Customs Clearance Area, International passenger terminal, Atlantic Wharf
81   P & O Ferries Passenger Lounge, Jamiesons Quay

82 Passenger Cruise Liner 'Argonaut'

83 *Kong Olav*, Norwegian Passenger Cruise Liner, Waterloo Quay

regular supplies of fuel, water, food, and a wide range of specialised equipment, drills, diving gasses, and chemicals etc. All have to be shipped out by sea on specialised supply vessels, and by the mid 1970s Aberdeen had become the principal offshore support harbour in Europe. Although there are no world-wide statistics available, by the 1980s Aberdeen Harbour was probably handling a greater tonnage of offshore installation traffic than any other port in the world.

Although regular liner traffic declined, Aberdeen Harbour retained a position of importance in handling bulk cargoes throughout the twentieth century. As coal traffic declined, so bulk oil and petroleum traffic increased so that by 1984 some 844,898 tonnes were being imported annually. Bulk minerals, fertilisers, and cement were imported in considerable quantity as well as steel pipes, steel casing, machinery, and oilfield equipment. Timber, paper and pulp had declined, but the new forest products terminal is expected to reverse the trend.

In the post World War II era, exports of bulk cereal changed from oats to barley, and a new trade was developed in export of scrap metal. Manufactured goods, especially oilfield equipment, dominated the export trade, and slow but steady progress has been made since 1970, so that overall an equal balance between inward and outward traffic has almost been achieved.

Passenger traffic after World War II was initially limited to the ferries

84 Passenger and Freight Ferry at the International Ro-Ro Terminal, Atlantic Wharf

serving Lerwick in Shetland. It was recognised, however, that since Aberdeen lay closer to Royal Deeside and to the Highlands than any other Scottish port, there was an advantage to be exploited by attracting cruise liners to the port. In the summer months, regular calls are now made by cruise liners, and a fleet of coaches whisks passengers away to the delights of Scotland's castles, mountains, rivers, and forests. For a while in the 1970s Norwegian passenger vessels undertook short shopping cruises to Aberdeen, and the close proximity of the harbour to the city centre shops was an advantage exploited by the passengers to the full. A passenger service to and from offshore installations proved successful for a period, and was found much more reliable than helicopters. This is a service which could well be again resumed with advantage.

Two attempts have been made to establish overseas ro-ro ferries to Aberdeen, but both were withdrawn after a short period. A passenger and freight service to Norway, Denmark, and the Faroe Islands was withdrawn for political reasons just at the point when traffic was beginning to develop. Another ferry for freight alone failed after only one month. This resulted from high running costs arising because the complex weekly schedule involved five ports—Aberdeen, Stavanger in Norway, Halmstad and Wallhamn in Sweden, and Aarhus in Denmark—a connecting service to/from US Gulf ports at Wallhamn only connected every other week, and traffic levels on this leg were quite insufficient. In spite of these two failures, there is still potential for development of ferry services, and recent studies show Aberdeen ideally placed for passenger ferries to and from Continental Europe—such a service would have a profound effect on tourism throughout Grampian and the Highlands.

Although the pattern of trade has changed over the nineteenth and twentieth centuries several common threads remain. Clearly, many of the deep-sea trades have been concentrated in large container ports in England, and much of the Continental traffic has been lured away to the English ferry ports. Completely new trades have been developed—offshore installation traffic, bulk fuel and petroleum products, being the two most important. Nevertheless, many traditional trades remain. Aberdeen still ranks amongst the largest fishing harbours in Europe, and is currently one of the three largest in the United Kingdom in terms of the tonnage of white fish landed. Passenger traffic is the second largest in Scotland, and traditional cargoes of grain, forest products, and manufactured goods still move through the harbour in significant quantities as do bulk ores and minerals. The modern port facilities should ensure that traffic will continue at a satisfactory level in the future, and surplus capacity will allow new trades to be developed.

Fishery Harbour

The official opening by Her Majesty the Queen of the new Commercial Quay West Fishmarket in 1982 marked the completion of a scheme of reconstruction of all the fishmarkets and associated quays in Aberdeen Harbour. It thus became an important milestone in the history of the Aberdeen fishing industry.

One can but guess at when fishing was first carried out at Aberdeen. It is likely that the prehistoric folk of 5000 BC included fish in their diet, and certainly a great quantity of shells and other marine deposits believed to have been from this age have been found in the harbour area on the former inches. Immigrants from continental Europe arriving some 3,000 years later almost certainly included fishing amongst their hunting activities, and succeeding generations caught salmon in the estuary of the Dee together with white fish close by offshore.

Written evidence of the fishing industry does not appear until the latter part of the thirteenth century. During the reign of King Alexander III Aberdeen had established a reputation as an exporter of fish, and as the small township grew, a reputation was established for high quality fish. In 1281 King Edward I of England sent agents to obtain provisions for his army preparatory to an invasion of Wales, and one Adam of Fuleham was commissioned to buy 100 barrels of salmon and 5,000 salt fish in Aberdeen. This suggests that Aberdeen was well versed in the art of fish curing long before it was reputedly discovered in Flanders. Records show that in 1290 fish from Aberdeen was sent to Yarmouth—at that time the capital fishing port of England—and was subsequently re-exported to Norway. The Town Council register of 9 May 1398 recalls that three persons were fined for selling fish improperly, and in 1441 the Town Council decreed 'that no flesher or other person buy any fish till they were brought to the market'. Fishing was, however, a relatively small activity in the harbour, and was confined to the river and to the sea in the immediate environs of the estuary.

Although the principal activity of the harbour at the time was purely commercial to serve the trading community, the export of locally caught salmon predominated amongst cargoes. The herring trade, for which

Aberdeen subsequently became famous, was non-existent except in the hands of Dutch fishermen who for centuries had been fishing for herring off Scottish coasts. In 1612, the City magistrates purchased and fully equipped a fishing vessel in Holland, and also engaged a Dutch skipper to train Aberdeen fishermen in the art of catching and curing the herring, but their scheme collapsed and the Dutch retained the monopoly working daily within sight of the shore. Occasionally there were protests about the large number of 'Hollanders' who also manned some of the local fishing boats belonging to the town, and some were even admitted to the Burgess Roll, but Aberdeen fishermen did not themselves make much attempt to fish far off shore, nor were they then much interested in the herring.

In those early years fish had to be compulsorily brought to the market for sale, and it was prohibited for fishermen to sell their catch privately. They were also prohibited in 1600 from fishing or selling fish on Sunday, and in 1610 this prohibition was extended to the gathering of bait on Sundays. The fishing community generally lived at 'Futtie', and according to Parson Gordon's map of Aberdeen in 1661, the fishermen's boats were berthed at 'Pockraw'—the present day Pocra. The eminent Parson also shows on his map the catching of salmon in the River Dee by net and coble, substantially the same method as used today.

The Town Council had always been closely involved with the fishing industry. The famous charter by King Robert the Bruce of 10 December 1319 gave certain fishing rights to the City, but these referred to salmon fishings. Subsequently, the Charter by King James VI of 17 July 1617, granted to the inhabitants

> of our said burgh, thorling water and fire within the same, all and whole Castlehill, the green meadow, the suburb called Futtie, with the chapels thereof, and all ferry boats and white fishings pertaining thereto

A similar grant was made by King Charles I in his Charter of 3 August 1631, but this later document throws rather more light on the area of fishing in those days:

> . . . other fishings whatsoever on the said waters of Dee and Don, and through all the bounds and limits thereof respectively set forth above, belonging and pertaining to our said burgh, and as they and their predecessors will want to possess the same, and with all other fishings as well as salmon as of white fish, in the salt water of sea between the said mouths of Dee and Don, and at the said mouths of the foresaid waters, on both sides thereof;

Present day readers will be all too well aware of the variations in the fortunes of the fishing industry, but it is interesting to note that there had been bad times long before. In 1659 the fishers of Futtie, to the number of thirty families, petitioned the Town Council for assistance since they were 'reduced to indigence by the total decay of their trade for many years'.

Prior to 1742, the fish market had been situated in Castle Street, but was then removed to the head of the old shore—probably at the foot of the Shiprow—where boats could be conveniently unloaded. In the Castlegate, there had formerly been an old fish cross, probably erected before 1561, which was eventually removed, and the fish was subsequently displayed for sale on the 'plane stanes'. Fish from other communities such as Cove, Findon, and Newburgh, was also sold here despite the provision of levelled ground and a shelter on the south side of the Shiprow.

Town records shed an interesting light upon the decision to remove the market to the Ship Row. The Aberdeen Council Register (Vol 61, p 52) of 21 April 1742 reads:

> The said day the Council taking to their consideration that the keeping of the Fish Mercat upon the publick Castle Street of the Burgh has been for thir many years past Complained upon as a publick nuisance and offencive to the inhabitants and strangers, and that the same could be remeeded by removing the said Fish Mercat down to the old shore of this Burgh, which would be a very convenient place for the boats to land there with their fish and could be alwise keeped clean, And the Council having gone and visited the said old shore, they were unanimously of opinion that the same was a commodious place for a fish mercat, and that if there were a breast of stonework built up and a stair under from the water, and all the ground levelled from the street, that the same would make a large compleat area for a Fish Mercat, and do unanimously agree that the same ought to be made out PROVIDING the Expence thereof do not exceed the sum of forty pound sterline money and in case the Magistrates can get workmen to contract for doing the said work at or under the said sum, then appoints the same to be instantly set about, and the Dean of Guild to defray the expense thereof.

A futher interesting note appears in the Dean of Guild Accounts of 1741-2:

> Item paid for stones and building a dyke at the fish merkat and laying and covering the causey thereof as per account and warrand £150 (Scots)

The Dutch monopolised the fishing off the Aberdeen coast, and in the early nineteenth century the French were also strongly in evidence. The French fishermen generally appeared during the middle of the summer remaining for two or three months often competing for the same fishing grounds as local fishermen. Locally it was argued that the French nets were of such construction as to injure fish and strong complaints were made. The first real attempt to establish deep sea fishing at Aberdeen was made about 1836 when a fishing boat of some seventy feet was built for the purpose. The local fishermen were, however, reluctant to go further afield and there was no real action until about 1870. In 1861 when a question arose in respect of the fishing convention with France, it was stated that 'the fishing carried on in the district of the port is on a small scale by a few natives'.

The earliest reference to the whale fishing industry in Aberdeen was in 1752 when a company was formed locally to fit out and send two vessels to the Greenland whale fishings in March 1753. The venture initially met with some moderate success, and the first voyage saw the first ship returning with five whales and the second ship with two whales. Between 1755 and 1763, the two vessels imported upwards of eight tons of whale fins and 350 butts of train oil or blubber, but in the following twelve years the trade ceased and the company was dissolved. The failure was reputedly due in part to the exigencies of war, although as far as possible every facility was granted to whaling vessels. They were exempted from the general embargo laid upon ships, and special measures were taken to protect the Greenland whale fishermen from impressment. These regulations did not always succeed, and it is recorded that in 1760 five seamen from the whaler *City of Aberdeen* were impressed.

Many of the early whalers were built in New England and had been constructed to carry from sixteen to twenty guns. In 1783, another whaling company was formed and two vessels, the *Hercules* and the *Latona* were fully equipped. Another vessel of some 400 tons was purchased in London but due to severe weather the ship was detained there until almost the commencement of the first whaling season. As a vessel of this burden could not enter or leave Aberdeen harbour at that time save at spring tides, some difficulties ensued. Later in 1787, a further whaling vessel was purchased and the magistrates were petitioned for the erection at Pocra Pier of suitable buildings for the manufacture of whale oil.

The whaling industry was pursued with varying degrees of success, and there was a steady increase in the number of Aberdeen vessels carrying out whaling in the waters off Greenland. In 1808, the total capture by Aberdeen vessels for the season amouned to 120 whales. By 1817 there were five companies established in the whaling trade in Aberdeen employing altogether fourteen ships of 4,379 tons, the number of hands on board amounted to 700. Each crew averaged fifty men consisting of a master, mate, surgeon, six harpooners, six boat steerers, six line managers, six landsmen, six apprentices and seventeen seamen.

From that date on the industry showed a steady decline, and twenty years later in 1857 Aberdeen possessed only two ships engaged in the trade. Whilst Aberdeen was declining, Peterhead was rapidly developing as a whaling centre to the detriment of Aberdeen which never regained its former prominence as a whaling port. Two Aberdeen whaling vessels the *Sophia* and the *Lady Franklin* owned by the Aberdeen Arctic Company were sent in search of Sir John Franklin the explorer who had failed to return from an Arctic expedition.

The old fish market at the foot of the Shiprow lasted for a remarkably long period of time. It is known to have stood at the foot of Market Street and Trinity Quay on part of the site now occupied by office buildings, and extended to the foot of the Shiprow. In 1834 a small committee was appointed by the Town Council to look into possible improvement, and a small amount of work was carried out. Subsequently in 1844 it is recorded that an application was made by Messrs Adam and Anderson, Advocates, to alter the level of that part of the Shiprow opposite the fish market. The Council agreed 'on condition that the Town be relieved of all expense

85   Construction of fish market building at Palmerston Quay, 1891

attending the same, as well as the expense of making a proper stair down to
the fish market, raising the front wall of the market and widening the foot
pavement opposite'. In 1851 there was an attempt to move the fish market to
the inches, but the rights of the proprietors of salmon fishings precluded any
action.

Problems began to arise as a result of complaints by local inhabitants and
by the owner of the nearby Douglas Hotel, and a new scheme of improvement was proposed. The cost of the proposals were estimated at £2,500, and
all the old familiar arguments were again heard. It was explained that the
revenue of the market had hitherto barely paid the annual charges and the
development could not be afforded. The matter was again revived in October
1860, and yet another committee was appointed to look into the matter.
More time elapsed but at the Council meeting on 5 November 1866 a very full
report was presented, and the Town's Superintendent of Works submitted
drawings of fish market sheds which were to be enclosed with a strong

86   Landing fish at Commercial Quay, c.1900

wooden fence. The buildings were to be of a temporary character due to the possible diversion of the River Dee which was being considered at that time. The report stated that the old market site had no frontage to Market Street, and suggested approaching the new market company for the purchase of the narrow strip of ground which lay between the site of the market and Market Street. Eventually the Council's offer of £440 was accepted, and this transaction proved to the advantage of the Council who subsequently in 1872 sold by public roup the solum of the market at a price of £2,910.18s. 9d.

The question of a new temporary market at the inches was again raised, and in August 1867 estimates amounting to £339.10s. 0d. were accepted for the erection of the new temporary market at the inches on the west side of South Market Street, adjoining the Deeside Railway. The ground which belonged to the Harbour Commissioners was let at an initial annual rental of £12.

Eventually this site was sold to the Great North of Scotland Railway Company. The new market was opened on 18 November 1867, and the market dues were let at an upset price of £25. By 1873 these dues were leased at £107, and a set of rules and regulations for guidance was drawn up. In 1871 further improvements were introduced when cement was laid down between the tables.

This new market was only intended to be of a temporary character, and rapidly became inadequate for the expanding trade. About 1864 a small screw boat, the *Deacon* had been the subject of trawling experiments, but the venture was a failure although trawling methods were being used with increasing success by sailing vessels. In 1868 the Aberdeen fishing fleet comprised one steamer of 26 tons, one lugger of 30 tons, 124 open boats of 10 to 16 tons, and 112 open boats from 3½ to 5 tons—a total of 237 sailing or row boats together with the one steamer. In 1882 the *Toiler* a paddle tug, built on the Tyne, was purchased in Dublin by an Aberdeen syndicate for £1,550 and renovated by the owners for trawl fishing. The vessel equipped with trawl gear left Aberdeen for her first trip on 21 March 1882, and fished mostly in Aberdeen Bay or close by the coast to the northwards. The experiment was a tremendous success and the catch for the first month realised some £207. A paddle steamer had obvious limitations, however, and s.s. *Bonita* was subsequently purchased and steam trawlers driven by screws were soon to be built in Aberdeen. The first locally built boat was the *North Star* built by John Duthie & Sons & Co with engines and boilers by Hall Russell & Co. This vessel was launched in September 1883 and up to May 1891 landed £46,591 worth of fish.

The advent of steam trawling and upsurge in landings rendered the

temporary fish market wholly inadequate. Catches from the early trawlers were discharged at a small wooden jetty at Point Law but when exposed for sale they were subject to inclement weather, and were contaminated by the dirt and mud. In the year 1885, the quantity of fresh fish landed at Aberdeen by vessels and boats direct from the fishing grounds was between 4,000 and 5,000 tons representing a value in excess of £56,000, and to this should be added herring and Shetland fish, the value of the former being about £55,000 and the latter over £2,000. Early success of trawling is evidenced in the large number of vessels built in Aberdeen. In September 1885, the Town Council remitted to the Finance Committee a further investigation of removing the temporary fish market and providing more commodious accommodation. Yet another sub-committee was appointed to carry out an investigation, and in their report to the Council on 10 January 1887, they said that they had visited London, Lowestoft, Yarmouth, Grimsby, Hull, Hartlepool, and Shields, finding that the most recently constructed markets were placed no more than 8 or 10 feet distance from the quayside. They recommended a suitable design, and put forward detailed proposals for a market along the side of the inches at what is now Commercial Quay.

The Scheme was to utilise ground belonging to the Harbour Commissioners, and plans were prepared showing a landing quay some 900 feet in length with a market 459 feet in length with a depth of 36 feet covering an area of 1,980 square yards, and the building sited some 10 feet away from the edge of the quay. The plans were for a building constructed of corrugated iron with sliding doors, and a portion at the west end was to be used for retail purposes with appropriate tables. Some twenty-one offices were to be erected for letting to fish dealers and salesmen at an annual rent of at least £7 with a rent of £5 for each of the stalls. The total estimated revenue was given as £537 and from this had to be deducted rent to be paid to the Harbour Commissioners for the site, attendants wages, and for repairs and other incidental charges, It was proposed that all fish should be landed at the fish market with the exception of herring. Some considerable arguments occurred subsequently when the fish merchants, curers, and salesmen together with the Torry fishermen lodged petitions suggesting the market should be placed on the south side instead of the north side of the basin, and after conferring with the Harbour Commissioners, and with all others interested in the fish industry a referendum was held. Some 407 voted for a fish market on the north side against 44 for the south side, and the present site of the market

facing page
87 Construction of Palmerston Quay Fish Market, 1892
88 Construction of fish market quays in Albert Basin, 1889–1894

was thus chosen by the vote of the practical men since the heavy vote of 287 fishermen predominated. The Harbour Commissioners agreed to the proposed rent of 9*d.* per square yard per annum subject to review at the end of five years.

Tenders were invited, and contracts awarded. An arrangement was entered into whereby the Harbour Commissioners were authorised to collect the dues payable to the Council on fish landed along with rates levied by the Commissioners. At 6 a.m. on 20 May 1889 the original market at Commercial Quay West was opened for business. Fifty vessels having arrived in the basin, some thirteen were moored at the new fish quay, and the *Lily* was the first vessel to take up quarters. Additionally there were several line boats so that accommodation was severely taxed and every spare inch of room was occupied. Had more line boats been in attendance, they would not have found space. The honour of driving the first bargain fell to Mr A J Tulloch. A more formal official opening subsequently took place on the same day at 11 a.m. in the presence of the Lord Provost, the Town Council, and Harbour Commissioners. Long speeches were made, which were followed by less formal celebrations by the fish wives which were later described as being of 'extraordinary hilarity'.

The 1889 market was a success from the outset, but from the opening day it was clear that it was already too small. There were many complaints, both about the lack of accommodation and about the depth, and the Council decided to extend the market eastwards for a distance of 240 feet at a further cost of £1,634.8*s.* 6*d.* In 1891 following representations from trawl owners, sales-

89 Divers preparing to salvage sunken trawler
    Loch Lomond, 1953

men, and others, it was decided to extend the market yet further towards the old graving dock, a distance of some 250 feet so as to give a total length of 1000 feet. In 1899 even more extension was considered necessary, and a development some 424 feet in length along Market Street with a width of 50 feet was agreed, the quay having already been built by the Harbour Commissioners in 1892. It was also decided to construct an administration centre for the market containing a Superintendent's room with stores, sanitary inspector's office, a telegraph office, a telephone room, and refreshment rooms. The expense was to be borne mutually by the Town Council and the Harbour Commissioners, and the cost was estimated at £8,000 exclusive of the cost to the Commissioners of extending and strengthening the wharf.

Despite all these extensions, market space was still proving inadequate, for the fishing industry was now at the height of a boom. In 1911 out of a total fleet of some 320 steam trawlers working from Scottish ports, 217 fished

90　Recovery of trawler sunk in Harbour

from Aberdeen. In 1891, some fifty-nine steam trawlers and five line fishing boats belonged to the port, and by 1893 the total number of fishermen belonging to the port employed in trawling and line fishing was 1,405. By 1910, there were 217 steam trawlers and fifty-three line fishing boats, and some 2,127 men were engaged on the trawlers alone.

In October 1902 an extension of 580 feet along Commercial Quay from Blacks Lane to the return wharf near the graving dock was approved with a width proposed of 51½ feet. Ten years later an extension of 400 feet along Albert Quay was agreed, and in 1928 the whole market was subject to a scheme of improvement and reconstruction, and the Commercial Quay side was extended another 300 feet to the eastwards on the site of the old graving dock, and the narrower parts were widened to make a universal width of 52 feet. Up to this point, the berthing space had been 2,295 feet, and it was now extended to 2,595 feet. The Town Council were still responsible for the buildings, but the Harbour Commissioners had carried out reconstruction of the quays at the same time at a total expenditure of £113,929. 2s. 5d.

Harbour improvements for the fishing industry were not merely confined to the provision of fish market space. In those far off days, the same principle applied as today, and vessels first landed their fish in the market and then moved to other quays in the harbour for servicing, repairs, and the taking of stores and ice. Following the diversion of the River Dee during the years 1870 to 1873, Torry Harbour was built in 1896 providing 624 lineal feet of quay space. This was largely used by the smallest type of inshore fishing vessel. Mearns Quay on the opposite side of the River Dee was constructed in two separate phases—the first between 1904 and 1906, and the second between 1914 and 1923. River Dee Dock on the south side was also built about the same time during the years 1909 to 1915, and provided 1,398 lineal feet of extra quay space which was partially devoted to the servicing of fishing vessels, and partially to the import of petroleum and petroleum products. In 1927, a goods shed latterly known as the 'Herring Market' was built at Mearns Quay and was largely used for imported dried fish. Albert Quay, used for servicing of fishing vessels, was completely reconstructed in 1932, and between 1931 and 1932 Commercial Quay fish markets were extended to a new face line.

It is of interest to note from Harbour Board records how the size of the fishing fleet has varied. The earliest detailed fishing records are in 1888 in which year there were 10,810 arrivals of fishing craft comprising 2,763 (25%) arrivals by trawlers, 296 arrivals by steam and motor liners (3%), and 7,751 arrivals of sailing and motor yawls (72%). These vessels between them landed some 6,659 tons of fresh fish. In 1914 Aberdeen achieved the

91　World record catch of halibut landed from steam line fishing vessel *Ellena*, 1950

92 HRH Princess Anne, accompanied by the General Manager, meets the crew of record breaking fishing vessel *Argonaut IV*

distinction of being the largest fishing port in the British Isles. The all-time local record landing occurred much later when in the year 1925 some 129,916 tons of fish were landed by fishing vessels. Trawler arrivals then amounted to 18,137 (83%), steam and motor line fishing vessels accounted for 1,679 arrivals (7%), and the balance of 2,139 arrivals comprised sailing and motor yawls (10%). By 1959 the pattern of fishing had been changed, and in that year some 99,411 tons were landed. Trawlers by this time accounted for 10,890 (91%) of the arrivals, steam and motor line vessels accounted for 436 (4%), and sail and motor yawls for 672 (6%). Although there was some subsequent improvement in total landings culminating in the post-war record of 118,627 tons of fish landed in 1970, by the year 1980, only 42,493 tonnes was landed in the full year, and this by a mere 4,823 vessel arrivals.

In 1957, the government appointed a Committee of Inquiry into the fishing industry nationally under the chairmanship of Sir Alexander Fleck, and their report was produced in January 1961. The committee examined every aspect of the fishing industry, and ports were given detailed attention.

At this particular time the four major ports of Hull, Grimsby, Aberdeen, and Fleetwood accounted for seventy-six per cent of all British landings. Of these four ports, the three English ports were all owned by the British Transport Commission who were consulted by the Committee in some detail. It was therefore somewhat surprising that the Committee did not take the trouble to confer with the port authority in Aberdeen which at that time was the third largest fishing port in Britain, and easily the largest in Scotland. Many Aberdeen fishing organisations were, however, individually consulted and the report concluded with a recommendation that a Working Party be set up to carry out a port-by-port investigation. It was suggested that grants and loans for the improvement of dock side facilities should be made available. Eventually, a Committee was set up under the Chairmanship of the Fisheries Secretary of the Department of Agriculture and Fisheries for Scotland to investigate the fishing facilities at Aberdeen Harbour. The Board were represented on this committee, which continued in existence between 1963 and 1965 but failed to make any recommendations of major importance. The market at that time was still owned by the city who were reluctant to dispose of the buildings to the Harbour Board. Discussions with the city authorities did, however, take place but no agreement could be achieved as to whether the aged fish market—now in its eighth decade of business—constituted an asset or a liability.

In May 1967 agreement was eventually reached to the effect that the Harbour Board would pay to the common good fund of the city the sum of £37,500 for the transfer of the market. Unfortunately, however, this agreement had been overtaken by events, and an examination by the Board's consulting engineers early that month had found 600 feet of the central section of Commercial Quay to be unsafe, and this was taken out of use on 12 May. On 15 May the Board gave instructions to prepare designs for a replacement of quay and market, and in October the same year a Joint Working Party was set up with representatives of the fishing industry and the Harbour Board to examine the whole question of fish market quays and buildings, and the most suitable form of replacement. The following year, 1968, a contract was let for the construction of a new quay to replace the 600 feet section which had been withdrawn, and construction started on 13 May. The work of reconstructing the quay was completed on 28 May 1969, and in accordance with the terms of the Aberdeen Corporation (Fish Market) Order Confirmation Act 1969, all the fish markets were transferred into the ownership of the Harbour Board on 25 June 1969.

The Board carried on to erect a new fish market building on the reconstructed quay, and grant aid was given by the Department of

Agriculture and Fisheries for Scotland amounting to one-fifth of the cost of the building. On 10 November 1971, the new fish market building came into use, and on the same day Palmerston Quay and fish market had to be taken out of use having also become unsafe. In the meantime, and arising from the deliberations of the Working Party, trials were instituted on 16 March 1971 of a pilot scheme for improved handling of the fish by a system of conveyors on the quayside. Sadly, agreement could not be reached between the Board and the industry as to the success or otherwise of the experiment, and the trials were called off in November.

Although 1970 had witnessed the handling of the largest post-war tonnage of fish in the harbour, there had been problems in regard to both port charges and the cost of unloading fish from vessels on to the quayside. A Public Inquiry into the Harbour Board charges was conducted in 1970, and as a result the Board, who desperately needed the money in order to implement a complete programme of fish market replacement, were compelled to accept the reduced rate of 2d. per pound sterling *ad valorem* on all fish landed. A more serious matter, however, was the question of fish handling costs in Aberdeen which alone in Scotland was, and still is, carried out by registered dock workers under the terms of the 1946 Dock Labour Scheme. The smaller inshore fishing vessels complained that the employers of the porters, the Fishing Vessel Owners Association, were treating them unfairly, and they objected to the exclusive use of dock workers and the high landing costs arising from the inclusion of Aberdeen within the National Dock Labour Scheme. They also complained at the unfair allocation of landing berths. As a result, the inshore fleet largely boycotted Aberdeen from around 1970, and for the most part commenced using the nearby port of Peterhead. This was a prime example of history repeating itself; as with whaling, Peterhead's gain was Aberdeen's loss. Some of these vessels eventually returned to Aberdeen attracted by higher prices paid for their catch. The demise of middle water trawl fishing due to increasing fuel costs, restrictions imposed by Iceland, Faroe, Norway etc, and by EEC quota regulations, resulted in the trawling industry drastically contracting, and thus without the previous support of the majority of the inshore fleet, the situation had been reached by 1980 in which the tonnage of fish landed was the lowest since 1898, and the level of landings has never fully recovered since.

Despite the discouraging reduction in fish landings, the Harbour Board still maintained faith in the long term future of the fishing industry in Aberdeen. Various administrative difficulties had to be overcome in obtaining government approval and grant aid, but nevertheless the difficulties were overcome, and a programme of complete reconstruction of the remaining fish market quays and buildings was put in hand, with both a new Palmerston Quay and Albert Quay and their respective fish markets coming into use during 1979. During the time all this construction was in progress, a serious crisis arose when the condition of Commercial Quay West deteriorated suddenly, and this had to be withdrawn from use on 1 April 1978 causing considerable difficulties in landing fish pending completion of Palmerston and Albert Quays.

With declining revenue from the fishing industry, it became harder than ever to justify the reconstruction of Commercial Quay West which comprised by far the largest part of the residual fish market. Eventually, with the promise of substantial grant aid from the EEC, and grant aid on a smaller scale from the UK government, the Harbour Board embarked on their greatest act of faith by commencing the final phase of reconstruction in 1980 at an anticipated cost of almost £3 million. The extent of this act of faith can be judged from the fact that in 1980 less than twelve per cent of the Board's total revenue came from the fishing industry. Cost of replacement of fishmarkets and quays now totalled some £5 million, and of this approximately £2 million had been provided by grant aid, the balance being funded by general harbour revenue. Additionally, in 1979 the Harbour Board replaced some 400 feet of quay in the River Dee at a cost of almost £1 million, and this is now used by smaller fishing vessels displaced from the former Herring Market section of Mearns Quay.

The rebuilding of Commercial Quay West and associated fish market was completed in 1982 which, by a happy coincidence, marked 100 years since the first steam trawling experiments by the *Toiler*. The Harbour Board were greatly honoured when HM The Queen, accompanied by HRH Princess Anne opened the new fish market on 5 August 1982. This happy occasion was a fitting conclusion to the complete rebuilding of Scotland's largest fish market with no less than 7,845 square metres of floor area.

Sadly the day of the large trawler is long past, and the Aberdeen fishing industry in the latter part of the century is but a shadow of its former self, and now contributes only about ten per cent of the Harbour Board's revenue on ships and goods. The Harbour Board pins its hopes for the future on the seine netters, and small inshore trawlers. Time alone will tell whether the Board's long term faith in the future of the Aberdeen Fishing Industry will be justified.

North Sea Oil and Gas

Few events have had a greater impact on the economy of North East Scotland than the discovery of oil and gas beneath the stormy waters of the North Sea. Similarly, the effect on both the infrastructure and the economy of Aberdeen Harbour itself far outweighs any other event in recent times.

The first seismic survey vessels made their appearance in Aberdeen Harbour in the early 1960s. With the passing of the Continental Shelf Act in April 1964 and the subsequent first round of licensing in September that year, momentous events were fore-shadowed. Some eighty-six areas or blocks of the North Sea were subject to the issue of drilling exploration licences in the Scottish area, and discussions between Aberdeen Harbour Board and the first of the oil companies commenced on 17 September 1964. This resulted in Shell UK Exploration & Production Company, on behalf of the Shell/Esso joint consortium, eventually leasing from the Board some ground at Torry as a storage yard, and entry was given at Whitsunday 1965.

Drilling in the sea bed necessitates substantial movement of material between shore bases and offshore drilling rigs. Apart from equipment and consumable supplies required on the rig itself, vast quantities of drilling mud are necessary throughout the operation in order to control pressure, to cool the drilling head, and to carry away waste material. Drilling mud largely comprising of barytes is thus shipped out to the oil rigs in dry powder form, and is mostly carried in bulk pressurised tanks located beneath the after deck of the supply ship. Additionally, vast quantities of steel casing are required together with cement for grouting the casing into position. A wide range of chemical additives must also be moved to the rigs together with drilling equipment, drill heads, diving gases, vast quantities of drill stems, and a wide miscellany of other matrial.

In addition food and other commodities must be shipped out to rigs and platforms to sustain drilling crews and other offshore workers.

Drilling mud and cement are generally stored at the Harbour in pressurised silos which are constructed on the quaysides, whilst most of the other material can be shipped from virtually any berth in the harbour. The first mud companies to become established in Aberdeen were British Ceca and

93 Oil rig supply ship *Tender Behanzin* turning in the Tidal Basin

IMCO in March 1969 closely followed by Dresser Magcobar. Within a short space of years, nearly a dozen silo installations were to be found in Aberdeen Harbour, and by 1973 there was a waiting list of incoming firms looking for suitable space.

A vast programme of drilling was carried out in the North Sea largely based upon the supply of material and equipment from Aberdeen Harbour. The first discovery was the Montrose Oil Field found by Amoco in September 1969, and the giant BP Forties Field was discovered in November 1970. The Shell/Esso joint venture made their first discovery with the Auk Field in February 1971, and this was closely followed by the discovery of the Brent Field in July of the same year. Hamilton Brothers discovered the Argyll Field in October 1971, and many further discoveries followed in rapid succession.

Use of the harbour by early drill-ships such as *Pelican* and *Glomar V* aroused much interest. These strange-looking vessels with their drilling derricks and helicopter platforms were unlike any other type of ship ever seen before, and they attracted large crowds to the quayside. Aberdeen Harbour, with its easy access from the sea, was an ideal base for drill-ships and support vessels of all types. Unfortunately, the navigation channel was too narrow to allow access by the much larger semi-submersible oil rigs.

In the very early days it became quickly apparent to the Harbour Board that no two oil companies adopted the same operating procedure, that many oil companies adopted a differing philosophy in regard to offshore support logistics, and these were generally seen to fall into three broad categories. Firstly, there were those oil companies who preferred to have their own

94 Drillship *Glomar V* in Aberdeen Harbour, 1973

private quay with adjacent storage areas, and over which they had complete autonomy and control. Other oil companies argued that available funds should be deployed wholly in the drilling operations out in the North Sea, and they therefore preferred to depend upon specialised service companies for the provision of support services and all quay facilities. A third, very small, group have been found to prefer operating through the common-user quays of the harbour without committing themselves either to the cost of operating their own local facility, or to dependence upon the facility provided by a service company under contract, latterly this traffic has increased greatly, especially by oil companies normally based in other ports.

From the outset, the Harbour management set about carefully ascertaining the detailed requirements of the oil companies, and within the constraints

95 Drillship Glomar V in Aberdeen Harbour, 1973

of their limited financial resources, they consciously set out to try and satisfy the individual requirements of each. At the time of the discovery of the first oilfields, most commercial traffic was handled in Victoria and Upper Docks where impounded water was maintained at a high level, but to which access could only be given through lock gates between two and three hours before and after high tide. Clearly this was of no use to the oil companies who from the outset demanded the ability to handle goods any time of the day or night, 24 hours per day, 365 days per annum. Tidal restrictions thus had no place in the operational scene. Clearly the lock gates had to be removed, and access to the enclosed docks be given irrespective of tidal conditions.

Most of they quays had been constructed in the previous century, and had the lock gates been removed and these quays exposed to the action of the tides, hydrostatic pressures would have been built up at the rear causing

96   Oil rig supply ship *Cumbria Service* at Chevron Oil Base

eventual collapse of the quays. The first step was, therefore, to reconstruct all quays within the enclosed docks. The Harbour Board did not have sufficient financial resources to fund this internally, and considerable difficulty ensued in obtaining suitable loan facilities as most of the financial institutions, having regard at that particular time to the financial collapse of the port of Liverpool and other major ports, regarded loans to ports as both risky and unattractive. Eventually loan facilities were granted by the British government under terms of Section 11 of the Harbours Act 1964, rates of interest were relatively high, and the loans were generally restricted to a ten year term. Eventually, however, work was put in hand and a major programme of quay reconstruction began.

At the time these new works were commenced, few envisaged that oil discoveries would follow on in such rapid succession, and offshore traffic consequently increased at a very rapid pace. During the period when many of the quays were immobilised during construction, congestion built up from time to time, and there were those who felt that the Harbour Board had

97 A submarine carrier/support vessel at Regent Quay West

attempted too much reconstruction at any one given time. The policy, however, soon proved to be correct, and within a relatively short period of intensive reconstruction work, it was possible to open the lock gates for the last time. In the intervening period, however, the original first generation of oil-rig supply ships which had been servicing the rigs in the early days of exploration were being replaced by larger vessels more suited to North Sea conditions. This necessitated a wider and deeper entrance to the Victoria and Upper Docks which had been originally designed to suit the hull form of sailing ships. A further scheme of reconstruction was therefore put in hand to widen the entrance to the former enclosed docks at a cost of £1¼ million, and once again more government money had to be borrowed, and the Board were fortunate in obtaining grant aid from the EEC Regional Development Fund—indeed they were amongst the first ports in the United Kingdom ever to obtain aid from this source.

By 1977 there were no less than seven exclusive oil supply bases in Aberdeen Harbour. Initial discussions with BP Petroleum Development Ltd had proved abortive as the Board were unable to provide new quay facilities

98   Oil rig supply ships at Waterloo Quay, 1983

quick enough for the company's requirements. Shell UK Exploration & Production Co Ltd, however, having already leased some harbour land, now leased the adjoining east side of River Dee Dock, and some limited reconstruction work was carried out in the mid 1970s to improve the quay structure. Amoco UK (Exploration) Ltd first discussed quay facilities in November 1971, and after a study carried out in February 1972, the Harbour Board gave their approval to the construction by Amoco of a complete new private quay adjoining the Board's own Pocra Quay. This new quay came into operation in December 1973/January 1974 by which time several other companies were also needing quay space. The management of the Harbour Board carried out an intensive marketing campaign, and in due course in 1974, Total Oil Marine Limited also commenced construction of a completely new quay for their own exclusive use at Torry, and the former North Boat ferry terminal at Matthews Quay was taken over in 1976 by Chevron Petroleum UK Limited following the transfer of ferry activities to the new ro-ro terminal. Texaco Ltd were perhaps the most fortunate in already having a quay in the River Dee for the import of petroleum products, and this was shared between the exploration and the distribution sections of the company. The number of privately operated oil company bases thus totalled five in all.

The majority of oil companies, however, preferred to utilise the facilities provided by specialised service base operators. Initially, two Scottish firms set about providing facilities in Aberdeen Harbour specifically to cater for these oil companies who were by now embarking upon a rapidly increasing programme of exploration for oil and gas in the North Sea. The John Wood Group had been long established in Aberdeen with fishing, shipbuilding and engineering interests, and had a large work force who already had many of the specialised technical skills required for the provision of base and servicing facilities. This company undertook partial reconstruction of the remaining two quays in River Dee Dock, and with the extensive adjoining facilities of the shipbuilding yard, they were able to provide full quay base facilities soon after the first discoveries of oil.

Seaforth Maritime Limited was formed in Aberdeen in 1972 to provide specialist facilities in the oil industry. In 1975 the company leased from the Harbour Board a section of the newly constructed Waterloo Quay East for use as a supply base providing three berths alongside. This company also built up their own fleet of supply ships and other offshore support vessels, and they soon acquired extensive local engineering and transport facilities in order to provide oil companies with comprehensive servicing similar to the Wood Group. Both Seaforth Maritime and the Wood Group operate their

bases on the 'one-stop shop' principle with silos on the quayside for mud and cement which are connected with manifolds on the quayside to which supply ships can connect their pressurised storage tanks. Both bases have fuel oil and fresh water supplies piped to the quay, and an oil rig supply ship can concurrently load bulk supplies of mud, water, cement, and fuel, whilst at the same time cranes provided from the Harbour Board's modern fleet of heavy duty mobile cranes can load the vessel with containers, tubulars, and the wide miscellany of supplies and equipment required in the offshore oilfield. Subsequently the Wood Group have constructed further quays in the River Dee to provide additional berths, and Seaforth Maritime have also provided an additional berth by the construction of a new quay on the site of the former North Lock.

Pocra Quay was originally built at the turn of the century and was mostly of timber pile construction. In the earliest days of offshore activity, a number of companies set up silo facilities at this quay which also had fuel oil supplies and water laid on. At that time no other quay in the harbour was thus equipped, and it was a natural development for this quay to be used from the earliest times in connection with offshore supply. Unfortunately, deterioration of the timber structure soon resulted in the quay edge becoming unsafe, and only limited dredging could be carried out without imperilling the structure. In the full knowledge that the quay was in urgent need of reconstruction, the Board only granted temporary tenancies to the many mud and cement companies set up in the area, and operations were carried out only with the greatest of difficulty.

A contract was awarded in 1982 for the reconstruction of the quay following removal of the old structure, and this work has now been brought to completion. The designed dredged depth is 6.5 metres below LAT (lowest astronomical tide), and the deck of the new quay is strengthened to permit access by heavy duty mobile cranes. Permanent installations have been built on the quay by a number of companies operating mud and cement silo facilities, and the fuel oil pipeline and water mains to the quayside have been replaced. This quay therefore now provides a first class facility to which all oil companies can have ready access. The quay is frequently used by oil companies based in other ports who have to send ships for specialised material only available in Aberdeen, and it is also heavily used by companies based elsewhere when chartering a supply ship from Aberdeen for single voyages out to oil rigs and platforms. Pocra Quay was re-opened as the eighth offshore base for common use by the Secretary of State for Transport

facing page
99 Unloading steel casing for offshore oil industry, Waterloo Quay

100   Opening of the ninth oil base at Mearns Quay by the Secretary of State for Scotland
accompanied by Mr G M Lawrence, Chairman of Aberdeen Harbour Board, 1984

on 6 May 1983. Some limited works remain to be carried out to strengthen
and deepen the quay linking the Amoco base at Pocra Quay, and in due
course the roadway at the rear of Pocra Quay will be renewed as funds
become available.

The port's ninth oil base was opened by the Rt Hon George Younger MP,
Secretary of State for Scotland on 4 May 1984. This quay replaced an old
timber and masonry quay known as the Herring Market, and which had been
withdrawn from use because it had become decayed and unsafe. The new
facility has been constructed to provide berths for two offshore support
vessels, and together with the adjoining open storage site has been leased to
Salvesen Offshore Services Limited who provide a service base facility
similar to Seaforth Maritime and the Wood Group. There are drilling mud
and cement silos on the quayside, fuel oil and water are piped to the quay,
and heavy duty mobile cranes can be used as at the other service bases. A
contract will be awarded in 1986 for the extension of this quay upstream in

101 Diving support ship *Shearwater Sapphire* at Atlantic Wharf

order to provide two additional berths, and Salvesen Offshore Services Ltd have meantime become a part of the Wood Group.

A specialist facility for training in offshore survival techniques was opened on the north side of the River Dee at North Esplanade East on 3 July 1980 by HRH The Prince of Wales, and is operated by Robert Gordons Institute of Technology. All types of offshore survival capsules and lifeboats are housed on the deck platform, and training is given to offshore workers in launching and handling techniques. The various craft are launched into the River Dee, and the crews then proceed to sea for training in boat handling in open water. The facility was one of the first of its kind in the world, and is the world leader in teaching new survival techniques.

Offshore safety vessels have been based in Aberdeen Harbour since the first programme of drilling commenced. Every offshore installation or oil rig must, by law, have a safety vessel in attendance close-by, and each vessel must have a capability of rescuing the survivors of any disaster. For the most part the earliest safety ships were converted fishing vessels, mostly painted conspicuous red or orange, and Aberdeen is home base port for the majority working in the Scottish sector of the North Sea. These ships are usually berthed in Albert Basin. Aberdeen Harbour has also become home port for a wide range of highly specialised vessels serving the offshore oil and gas industry. Diving support vessels, and other craft employing advanced technology such as the ships carrying both manned and unmanned submarines, are regular visitors to the harbour. Aberdeen alone has full support facilities for these remarkable ships.

Following the first discovery of oil and gas in the North Sea, Aberdeen very quickly established itself as the offshore oil capital of Europe, and has retained the title ever since. To achieve and to maintain this title the Harbour Board, Aberdeen City, and Grampian Region, have together combined with local companies and organisations to provide very specialised facilities for the new and developing industries. The presence of a highly skilled and responsible workforce with a good record of industrial relations was readily available. Excellent technical educational facilities were already well established in Aberdeen, and there were good road and rail links together with an airport. These and many other facilities such as development of industrial estates were all moulded to the requirements of the new industry. By the beginning of 1985, there were some 800 firms in the Grampian Region wholly involved in the offshore oil and gas industries employing some 50,000 people. Additionally many other firms have some measure of offshore involvement so that there would be 65,000 or more oil dependent jobs in the Region.

Development continues apace in both Aberdeen City and in the Grampian Region, and Aberdeen Harbour likewise continues a constant process of development and improvement. Despite the fact that the Harbour has surplus capacity, and is well fitted to handle present needs of the oil industry, further improvements continue to be made. New facilities have recently been made available in the Harbour for reprocessing of oil-based drilling mud and there is space in the River Dee to build more berths for offshore services or for commercial traffic. Changes in offshore technology are constantly monitored, and matching port facilities are provided wherever the demand arises.

Cargo and Fish Handling

No treatise on the history of any port or harbour would be complete without reference to the remarkable development of cargo handling techniques over the centuries. Sadly, little is known of earliest methods, but some Mediterranean civilisations developed quite remarkable techniques for the handling of stone blocks and other heavy lifts more than 4000 years ago. It has been facetiously suggested that Julius Caesar was the inventor of the modern sea container when he carried chickens and other livestock as provisions for his invading army when he crossed the Channel from Gaul!

There are no records of cargo handling in Aberdeen until the middle ages. From knowledge of early shipping and cargo handling techniques elsewhere, it must be assumed that great reliance was placed upon manual handling without recourse to any specialised equipment. When the Vikings raided Aberdeen, their long boats were drawn up on the beach, and their plunder was lifted aboard by hand piecemeal, and when they subsequently returned on more peaceful trading missions, the same technique was used in reverse. Fish, like general cargo, was handled manually with small fishing vessels landing at the beach and passing their catch over the side in creels or strung together. It has to be remembered that these early trading and fishing vessels were very small indeed. Early fishing vessels were strictly limited to working close inshore and in the estuary, and they probably did not exceed 20 feet in length, and trading vessels until about 1400 were probably around 50 feet with a maximum length of around 150 feet.

As cargoes became larger, and Aberdeen's importance as a trading centre increased, ships also became larger and different handling techniques had to be evolved. It is recorded that in 1273 Aberdeen was already an important exporter of ox hides, wool, salmon, oak boards, deer hides, lamb skins and similar goods. The larger vessels would have lain at anchor in the 'gawpuyll'—the tidal basin lying between Footdee and Torry—and their cargo would have been transferred piecemeal by hand into small rowing boats which carried the cargo up the narrow channel to the 'townheid'. The smallest trading vessels might possibly have been able to reach the townheid quay on spring tides, but they would have lain aground for a large part of the time they were being unloaded or loaded.

The use of lighters or 'keills' as they were locally known, carried on until the eighteenth century. For the most part small vessels would hand their cargo piecemeal over the side to the keills, but as ships became larger with a higher freeboard, then it would be necessary to hoist goods up out of the holds and lower them over the side in case of imports, and with the operation reversed for exports. To assist in this process, a pulley block was generally attached to the outboard yardarm of a square rigged vessel, or to the gaff or boom of a vessel with fore and aft rig. A rope was rove through this, and goods could thus be lifted into or out of the hold and into and out of lighters. Clearly, however, only small units of light weight could be so handled.

In the Middle Ages cargoes generally comprised goods packed in bales, barrels, bags, or else the cargo would be loose in bulk. A remarkable array of commodities was packed in barrels including salt, salmon, salted beef, tar, butter, gunpowder, peas, apples, onions, pipes, tobacco, alum, wheat. Bags were used for meal and for certain cereals, and 'bolles' or bales were used for textiles, and wool which was sewn up in hessian in packs roughly corresponding to the maximum weight a man could carry. Timber was handled loose, cargo was stowed aboard ships piece by piece, and unloaded the same way. Formerly it was very unusual to collect together a large number of boards in a single hoisting, and each piece was generally handed out of the ships hold to men stood on the deck who again passed the timber across to the quay or down into a keill. The process was both slow and arduous. Cargoes such as coal, lime, iron ore, and occasionally wheat were generally carried in bulk. The loading process carried out at a quay often utilised wheelbarrows which were pushed down a gang plank, and the contents were roughly tipped into the hold where trimmers spread the goods out toward the extremities. An alternative method was to carry the goods on board in bags, and either to open the mouth of the bag and tip the contents into the hold, or else to rip the bags and bleed the contents into the hold. It is interesting to note that this method is still in use in some less developed parts of the world even today, and the writer recalls endless battles with Asian stevedores at remote anchorages in the Far East. Loading ore into a modern ship by this primitive technique was slow in the extreme, and extremely inefficient in view of the difficulties in trimming the cargo out to the ends and the sides of the hold.

The first crane was erected in Aberdeen harbour in 1583 by David Endeaught. The builder was initially allowed 1s. 6d. per tun for goods handled by the crane, but he made such a substantial profit on this that the concession was later redeemed, and the town charged 3*d*. per barrel which was the source of very considerable profit at that time to the harbour works. Around 1637–8 a second crane was required, and the original crane was thoroughly overhauled with new timber work, ropes, and pulleys. Movement of goods on the quay was generally by carriage on the back of a porter, one bag or one bale at a time, but for blocks of granite and other heavy goods, barrows were occasionally used or sleds. These latter comprised two wooden runners, sometimes with iron facing on the underside, and were either pulled by teams of men or by horses. Interestingly, similar sleds were in use at the riverside quays in the port of Antwerp until around 1960. Carts were also used, but the earliest versions did not have wheels, and comprised two poles secured to a box into which the cargo was tipped or placed. It has to be remembered that cargoes were themselves relatively small in volume, and in the seventeenth century an average size cargo would approximate 40 tons. To get a measure of the extent of trade of the harbour, from 1596 detailed accounts have been preserved showing the charges raised on each individual commodity which is itemised. In that year (1596) there were sixty-nine inward general cargoes, ten inward timber cargoes, and nineteen cargoes were loaded outwards. In short, there were less than two ship arrivals per week over the whole year—this compares with around 11,000 per year at the time of writing.

Very little progress was made in cargo handling technology either in Aberdeen or elsewhere in the course of the next few hundred years, and in point of fact throughout the era of sail, the loading and unloading of ships cargoes was abysmally slow, and labour intensive. Towards the middle of the nineteenth century improvements became evident, many ships were equipped with winches so that instead of lifting one or two bags out of a ships hold, hoistings of five to ten bags could be lifted. Improvements in rigging for cargo handling were also effected. Some ships used one yardarm to plumb the quayside with another yardarm braced over so that a pulley would plumb the ships hold—this was the forerunner of the union purchase system which is still in use. For the most part, however, a single block was used on the outboard yardarm, and the hook was hauled back on board with a bullrope which was then secured to a cleat on the offside of the hatchway. This bullrope usually had a shackle or a pulley around the lifting fall (hoisting rope), and so, as the weight of each load of cargo was taken, it was steered up through the centre of the hatchway by keeping tension on this outboard bullrope. As the hoisting reached sufficient height to clear the coamings, the bullrope was slackened off, and because the (pulley) block on the yardarm plumbed the quay, the hoisting of cargo swung over toward the quay as the

102   Unloading cargo by steam crane, Upper Dock, 21 February 1900

bullrope was slackened off. The cargo was then lowered so that the hoisting of cargo landed on the quayside or in a lighter. The same arrangement worked in reverse for loading the ship.

The handling of fish made virtually no progress until the advent of steam trawling. Fish was invariably manhandled in creels or other forms of basket out of the fish room, and the creels were passed ashore by hand. The system did not change greatly until steam trawling saw the introduction of larger vessels, and quicker means of handling had to be adopted. A system based on the same principle as that worked on sailing ships was used, and has changed but little to the present time. The boom or derrick was set to plumb the quayside, and a pulley block was attached to this in precisely the same way as the block suspended from the yardarm of a square rigged sailing ship. The method persists to this very day, and has changed only to the extent of using an electric winch which replaces the steam winch of the steam drifter or trawler, and this in turn had replaced the wholly manual operation of the ropes by the vessels crew.

With the advent of steamships, changes came about rapidly in the type of equipment used. The earliest steamships had auxiliary sails, and on these ships, the yardarms could be used for handling cargo. As sails disappeared, an alternative had to be found, and the ships derrick took the place of the yardarm. Derricks were normally operated in pairs, with one derrick plumbing the ships hold, and another plumbing the quayside or lighter. This usual arrangement was known as a 'union purchase', and that derrick which plumbed over the ship side continued to be known as the 'yardarm'. Sometimes a single derrick was used but this usually necessitated manual handling of guys, and was generally slower than the union purchase method which enabled speeds up to twenty or thirty hoistings per hour to be attained with skilled winch drivers.

The advent of the largest clipper ships in Aberdeen toward the middle of the nineteenth century followed upon the enclosure of Victoria and Upper Docks, and the provision of a static water level at all states of the tide. This enabled larger ships to lie alongside quays so that there was no need of lighters, but little progress was made in the manner of handling cargo on the quayside. Some cargoes, such as timber, were landed into a stack on the quayside, and this was then delivered to the eventual receiver after the ship had departed. Other cargoes were often taken away by horse and cart, by the use of sleds, then by horse and cart, and latterly by motor lorry. The shore porters were, however, still carrying cargo away from the quayside well into the twentieth century, and sometimes this was carried out singly, in pairs, or in larger teams.

With the provision of transit sheds on the quayside, some cargo was moved, on wheelbarrows, or on porters trucks, or even manually, into these covered sheds where the goods were stored pending distribution to the inland receiver. Export cargoes were similarly received direct into a transit shed from a horsedrawn cart, and latterly by lorries or rail waggon. The goods were then transferred across the quay, and loaded into the ships hold where great expertise was necessary to ensure that goods were stowed, then as now, in such a manner as to avoid damage during the sea journey. The cargo for each port also must be stowed so as to be accessible in a proper order of rotation according to the various ports of call. Careful regard also had to be given to ships stability, and the ships officers had to calculate the trim and stability of a ship in order to provide the optimum sailing conditions. Clearly, a ship with too much weight at the bottom would act like a pendulum, and in heavy seas would tend to roll in an exaggerated manner with almost a whiplash effect. Conversely, a vessel in which too much weight was stowed in the upper part could become unstable, and the ship would capsize as it would not have the reserve stability to recover from rolling caused by the sea.

The very high cost of constructing steam ships necessitated efficient and

103   Unloading bags from quayside transit shed for delivery by steam lorry, *c*.1897

104   Cargo stored in goods transit shed, *c*.1910

105 Receiving export goods into cargo transit shed, *c*.1910

106 Unloading bag cargo, *c*.1910

economic operation of the very expensive capital asset, and very strong pressures soon became evident to minimise ship turn-round times in port. the argument is still advanced that a ship only earns money whilst the propeller is turning, and that every day spent in port represents a financial loss to the shipowner. With larger holds, and consequently larger cargoes, economic pressures soon developed so that a rapid turn-round of a ship in port became essential. Where it was previously acceptable for a sailing ship to take a month to unload a cargo of Canadian timber, this was no longer so in the case of an expensive steamship, and speed of cargo handling became all important.

Many of the larger ports faced serious labour problems, and labour was in general less inclined to co-operate in the interest of productivity. Aberdeen, in common with many ports of similar size, escaped the worst excesses of these problems, and for the most part the men engaged in handling cargoes were well known to one another, and anyone who did not pull his weight as part of a team could expect little sympathy from his colleagues, and was only given work by the supervisor when no one else was available. The larger ports were much more impersonal, and the old slow working tempo was much more difficult to improve. Conversely, in the very small ports, the irregular arrival of ships meant that there was no regular labour force to deal with cargo, and casual labour had little opportunity to develop skills.

The size of ships derricks and the lifting capacity of ships winches increased steadily from the beginning of the century, and at the time of the 1914–18 war, ships derricks generally varied between a one ton and a three ton safe working load, so that in union purchase they could lift little more than one ton hoistings of cargo. By the time of the second world war, most ships derricks had a lifting capacity of around five tons and a very large number of ships had special heavy lifting derricks which in some cases had a capacity of up to 150 tons. These very heavy derricks were slow and cumbersome to operate, and were reserved for single occasional heavy lifts. Ships derricks had also become much more adaptable, and could either be used at low capacity and higher speed in union purchase, or a heavy lift purchase could be attached for handling heavy pieces of cargo. Bulk cargoes continued to demand the use of shovels in the ships hold, and cargo was shovelled into steel skips which were then swung ashore, and the content tipped into vehicles.

Although the first crane had been introduced into Aberdeen harbour in the sixteenth century, and had been replaced by a succession of others over the succeeding years, these were generally manually operated. According to harbour plans of 1876 there were ten fixed cranes in the enclosed docks. One

107 Shear legs used for handling heavy lifts and for installing boilers and fitting out new
     ships' North lock c.1910

3 ton capacity crane was located at Upper Quay, there was one crane of 1 ton capacity at Regent Quay, and four cranes from 1 ton to 10 tons lifting capacity at Waterloo Quay together with four cranes at Blaikies Quay ranging from 1½ to 7 tons capacity. Toward the end of the century, however, steam cranes were introduced. The first steam crane was purchased in 1881 from Messrs Thomas Smith Limited of Rodley, near Leeds, at a cost of £374 and these useful appliances only went out of service after the 1939–45 war. Often capable of handling quite heavy lifts, these

108   Coastal collier unloading coal, Upper Dock, *c.*1937

109   Unloading grain by portable suction plant, 1950

cranes were generally very reliable, but demanded constant stoking of the boiler. There had to be occasional breaks for refuelling and watering, and also to remove the ash and clinker in order to give a good draught to keep the boiler going during the course of the working day.

Wooden shearpoles with 75 ton lifting capacity had been first erected in the nineteenth century adjoining the north lock for the fitting of ships engines, and also for occasional cargo heavy lifts. Eventually replaced by steel shearpoles of 100 tons capacity in 1910, these were finally taken down in 1975.

Modern luffing electric cranes were erected at Pacific Wharf in 1949, but fixed jib electric cranes had been installed on the roof of the former Regent Quay goods shed some years earlier. Since earliest times, there has been a steady increase in the lifting capacity of cranes so that the first electric 1 ton cranes and 1½ ton cranes mounted on the roof of the former Regent shed eventually became obsolete and steadily declined in use until they had to be removed. These cranes also had the disadvantage that the jib was fixed in one position, and could not be raised and lowered—an action known as luffing. Of the modern electric quay cranes, all are capable of luffing at the same time as cargo is hoisted and swung. This makes for a very fast operation. The initial cost of electric quay cranes is, however, extremely high, but in the long term they are more economic as they outlast most other crane types. There are some seven electric luffing cranes in the modern Aberdeen Harbour with lifting capacities from 6 to 50 tonnes.

Generally, diesel driven mobile cranes are around one-sixth of the cost of an equivalent electric crane of similar lifting capacity, but they only have one-third of the life-span of an electric crane. Their advantage is perhaps in that with a short replacement programme, each new replacement crane can take account of changes in cargo handling technology, and embody new features. An electric crane is, however, bought for a prolonged period of service and cannot be much changed. Against this, an electric crane is generally marginally faster than a mobile crane, is more reliable, has less maintenance costs, and generally has much better outreach clearance over a ships bulwarks.

Since the mid 1950s, the process of cargo 'unitisation' has rapidly progressed. During the war years 1939–45, forklift trucks were introduced, and limited use was made of pallets with cargo being stowed on these in the transit sheds for movement to and from the ships side. The next step came in the mid 1950s when cargo was moved on pallets, the goods remaining on the

facing page
110   Unloading cargo at Regent Shed using electric roof cranes

same pallet throughout the sea journey in the ships hold, and this consequently demanded a new breed of forklift truck capable of working on board ship. At the same time some cargo unsuited to palletisation was placed on board with the slings remaining around the goods throughout the sea voyage. Clearly this greatly increased the speed of turn around and reduced the demand for labour.

As mentioned earlier, the sea container is by no means a modern invention. Containers for regular shipment of freight by sea did not, however, come into wide spread use until after the 1939–45 war. Even during the war years, rudimentary containers were used for handling highly pilferable cargo, explosives, and other goods requiring special protection. It was in the 1960s that international standard sized containers appeared with a cross section 8 feet by 8 feet, and with lengths initially of 6 feet, 8 feet and 10 feet, but later standardising at 20 feet and 40 feet. The early use of containers allowed goods to be stowed safely in a container at point of origin inland. The goods were then untouched until reaching final destination after the sea voyage. The contents were thus provided with protection against pilferage throughout whilst at the same time allowing up to 35 tons of break bulk cargo to be moved quickly in one lift. The advent of the international standard container and the cellular container ship was a giant step forward in cargo handling, but this technique was never a very large scale feature at Aberdeen harbour.

The container did, however, have a serious effect on the trade of Aberdeen since many shipping companies built very large cellular container ships which were then based on perhaps one large British terminal port, and one large continental terminal. The direct trade to Canada, the US Gulf, and much other traffic was thus lost by both Aberdeen and other Scottish ports to other ports in the south of England nearer to the main trading routes, and where the greatest concentration of cargo was to be found.

Another fundamental change in cargo handling techniques had long been in course of development, and first became a feature of Aberdeen Harbour in 1977. Drive-on/drive-off (generally known as ro-ro) ferries had been in use on the Rivers Mersey, Thames, and Clyde, the Pacific Coast of Canada, and in many other parts of the world long before the 1939–45 war. The new use of converted landing craft after the 1939–45 war with ferry services carrying freight to Ireland and to the Continent from Britain were the fore-runners of the modern ro-ro vessel. Nowadays there are a great many such services connecting Britain with Continental Europe, Scandinavia, and

facing page
111   Modern cranes at Waterloo Quay

Ireland, and destinations even farther afield. Some of the larger ro-ro vessels now operate on world-wide services.

The first ro-ro ferry terminal in Aberdeen was constructed for P & O Ferries to replace their conventional service to the Northern Isles of Shetland and Orkney, and the first vessel, mv *St Clair* entered service in April 1977. This ship, with accommodation for some 700 passengers, also has a large freight and car deck so that lorries and passenger cars can be driven straight on board over a ramp built into the ferry terminal complex at Jamiesons Quay. Full supporting facilities were constructed to provide a passenger terminal, and large marshalling areas for cars and lorries. Where a shipper requires to move less than a full trailer load of freight, the goods can be consolidated onto one trailer along with other consignments, and this consolidation work is carried out in special purpose-built transit sheds adjoining the ferry terminal. There are also lairages, and both sheep and cattle can be carried on special trailers upon which is superimposed a livestock pen.

Sometimes the whole lorry goes aboard ship complete with driver, and sometimes a detachable semi-trailer is taken aboard by a special tugmaster tractor, and the unaccompanied traffic is collected at the other terminal port by another commercial driver.

Aberdeen Harbour Board introduced a second ro-ro terminal in 1979. The Aberdeen Eurolink is a floating ro-ro pontoon which can be used virtually anywhere in the harbour and was originally of unique design. This terminal can be used in conjunction with the international passenger terminal at Atlantic Shed, where the west end of the ground floor of the Transit Shed has been converted for use by passengers. Closeby is a covered Customs inspection bay for cars and for freight vehicles, and an adjoining high security compound for valuable trailer loads.

Much progress has been made in other forms of cargo handling in Aberdeen Harbour in the course of the last few years. There are bulk terminals for fuel oil, aviation spirit, and other petroleum products which are pumped ashore from tankers. There are facilities for handling calcium carbonate, slurry, and also dry powders such as cement from tankships, and in each case this is pumped into silos located on the quayside, or closeby, connected by pipeline.

Bulk cargo is no longer handled by the primitive method of shovels and buckets, but modern heavy-duty grabbing cranes have been provided so the cargoes of barytes, bentonite, coal, pumice, salt, and fertilisers can be grabbed out of ships and loaded straight in to waiting road vehicles. In reverse, bulk cereals grown in North East Scotland are brought to the harbour by road transport, and are loaded aboard ships using modern high capacity powered conveyors. Scrap steel is also exported from Aberdeen using high capacity steel skips which are loaded aboard a vessel with heavy duty cranes, and the contents tipped straight into the ships hold.

Cargo handling techniques have changed beyond all recognition in recent years. The very high cost of modern ships combined with modern trading methods demands that ships are turned round at minimum cost, and above all in minimum time. The days when sailing ships could lie in the harbour for one or two months to unload a cargo from distant parts have long since passed, and there have been greater changes in cargo handling techniques in the last twenty years than there have been in the preceding 200 years. This process of change in likely to continue, and it will be necessary for future Port Managers to be familiar with changing technology, and to continue to anticipate change thus ensuring Aberdeen remains to the forefront.

Dock Labour

There can be few matters in any port or harbour which evoke more controversy than the subject of dock labour, and there are few subjects upon which there is so much emotive and misinformed commentary. To understand the background in Aberdeen requires some general appreciation of the national dock labour scene spanning the last 100 years. Sadly, few of the critics of the present National Dock Labour Scheme have but the barest and most rudimentary knowledge of the Scheme, how and why it came into being, and its relevance to Aberdeen.

The central problem of dock labour, in a nutshell, lies in matching sufficient labour to a widely varying demand which in its turn arises from uncertain and irregular ship arrivals. Trading variations, tides, weather conditions, the national economy, all play their part in creating a situation unmatched in any other industry.

Since earliest times, cargoes were loaded into, or unloaded from, ships either by their own crews, crews assisted by some local labour, or entirely by local labour recruited on a day-to-day basis in accordance with demand. During the middle ages in Aberdeen, from the 14th century and for the following four or five centuries, the numbers of ships arriving in the harbour were sparse, and there was no justification in maintaining a large permanent labour force. When a ship arrived in the harbour, most of the stevedoring work on board the ship would be undertaken by the ship's crew unless the ship belonged to Aberdeen in which case the shipowner probably had a nucleus of local men who would undertake the work for him—generally under the direction of a ship's officer or a shorebased manager with seafaring experience.

In 1498, during the reign of King James IV, the Shore Porters Society was established, being then known as the 'Pynours', which may well have been derived from the French word for a bundle carried by a traveller. The Shore Porters were undoubtedly used to assist in the loading and unloading of shipping, but it seems likely that they were rarely engaged to work on board ships, but only undertook the 'porterage'—i.e. the handling of goods on the quayside. In some ports today the work undertaken by dockers on board ship is still known as 'stevedoring', and the work undertaken by dockers on the quayside known as 'porterage'.

The Charter granted by Queen Anne to the Shore Porters in Aberdeen in September 1707 contains the following references:—

> . . . to look after the shipping on behalf of the Merchants and the whole community thereof in all time comming and forever.

> . . . and ordain the foresaid Pynour Craft and their successors in all time comming to be Porters and Carriers (Warkmen) at the Shoar of our Royal Burgh of Aberdeen with liberty and privilege of burdening and discharging boats and other vessels whatever.

Arrangements for the handling of cargo in Aberdeen continued with little change until the early part of the twentieth century. By this time forces were at work elsewhere which were to have, in due course, a profound effect on Aberdeen as well as upon all other Scottish ports.

Until 1887, trade union organisation had not extended to the vast numbers of unskilled or partially skilled dockside workmen concentrated in London, Aberdeen, and other major ports. Older trade societies and artisan workers associations tended to keep aloof from unskilled labourers such as dock workers. The first effort at organisation culminated in the famous London dock strike of 1889 when the dockers' hero, Ben Tillett, fought long and hard to have the hourly rate of 5d. raised to 6d.—famed as the 'dockers tanner'. The London Dock Directors eventually conceded almost all the men's demands, and the Dock Wharf and Riverside Labourers Union was formed; rival societies sprang up in Liverpool, Glasgow, Belfast, and in other ports. By 1907 there were some 150,000 organised dock labourers throughout the country.

Casual employment of dock labour continued to trouble the ports. In 1920 a Commission of Inquiry was set up under the chairmanship of Lord Shaw of Dunfermline who roundly condemned the casual employment of dock labour arguing that it was a cause of poverty, degradation and inefficiency. The report comments as under:

> Labour frequently or constantly under employed is injurious to the interests of the workers, the ports and the public and it is discreditable to society. It undermines all security and is apt to undermine all self-respect on the workers part . . . If men were merely spare parts in an industrial machine, this calous reckoning might be appropriate. But society will not tolerate much longer the continuance of the employment of human beings on these lines. A system of casualisation must, if possible, be torn up by the roots. It is wrong.

There could hardly have been a clearer mandate for reform.

In simple terms, the old casual system allowed an employer to engage men for a day or a half-day to match variable labour requirement brought about by irregular ship arrivals. This fluctuating demand is at the very nub of the problem. Even today, in Aberdeen harbour there can be a shortage of fifty men one day and a surplus of fifty men the next day. There can be seventy ship arrivals one day and only one the next. Neither the employer nor the employee has any control whatsoever over these fluctuations in demand, but the importer, the exporter, and the shipowner all, understandably, demand that when the ship arrives in port there is sufficient labour to unload the cargo, or if the ship is loading exports, then they naturally demand that these be loaded without delay. In general, however, the importer, the exporter, and the shipowner do not have the worries of paying men to stand idle on those days when there are few ships in a harbour, and there are too many men for too few jobs.

The problem becomes more difficult in smaller ports, and as recently as the 1960s the National Association of Port Employers told Lord Devlin that decasualisation of the dock labour force would be impracticable in some

112   Steam crane loading granite blocks for export, Upper Quay c.1900

nineteen ports—including Aberdeen. They argued that because of the small labour force and the very wide fluctuation in trade, the use of casual labour was a pre-requisite. Certainly in a larger port employing many thousands of dock workers, it is much easier to overcome the problem of shortages and surplus of labour, especially where the individual cargo handling work is not mechanised and is labour intensive. In a modern context, however, with highly mechanised cargo handling and infinitely greater productivity, shortage of a relatively small number of men can cause profound delays to shipping.

Several early attempts were made to regularise port labour in all the larger ports including Aberdeen, and to introduce a scheme of registration as a first step toward abolishing complete reliance on casual labour.

Simple registration schemes were first introduced during the first world war, including such a scheme in Aberdeen. Mostly these schemes did not survive the return of the servicemen after the war, but following the Shaw Inquiry in 1920, attempts were again made to effect registration in all ports. In 1930 a Committee of Inquiry on Port Labour was appointed by the Minister of Labour to enquire into employment and unemployment in the ports of Great Britain with special reference to de-casualisation, and the administration of the unemployment insurance scheme as applied to ports.

113   Loading coal bunkers to steam trawlers, Albert Quay Coaling Installation 1951

That Committee, of which Sir Donald McLean was Chairman, emphasised the need for an efficient system of registration. By 1937 only Aberdeen and Glasgow were holding out against registration, and the Minister of Labour appointed yet another committee comprising Sir James Leishman and T Murray Taylor under the Chairmanship of J M Irvine KC to investigate the circumstances giving rise to the special difficulties in Glasgow and Aberdeen. In their final report they put forward special proposals to the Port of Aberdeen Labour Employers Association on the one hand, and to the Aberdeen Branch of the Transport and General Workers Union (Dockers Section) on the other. No recommendation was made for the regulation of licensed porters at the fish market, who were employed by the Aberdeen

114   Timber stacked by hand at Pacific Wharf, 1955

Steam Fishing Vessel Owners Association, as they were not deemed to be 'engaged in operations recognised as dock labour'.

The Irvine Report of 1937 gives a clear portrayal of the casual nature of dock labour in Aberdeen. The report describes the method of engagement of labour in the following terms:

> Under the Wage Agreement, which has operated since June, 1924, the 'working day' is from Monday to Friday 8 a.m. to 12 noon-1 p.m. to 5 p.m., and on Saturday 8 a.m. to 12 noon. The minimum engagement is for a half-day, that is, from 8 a.m. to 12 noon or from 1 p.m. to 5 p.m. There are no recognised calling-on places where men seeking employment present themselves for engagement. The engagement of labour takes place at the ship-side at 7.45 p.m. and 12.45 p.m. A number of dock workers are in use to congregate at Regent Bridge—a bridge which separates the Victoria Dock from the Upper Dock—and at Commercial Street. Foremen who experience a shortage of labour at the ship-side occasionally go to one or other of these places for additional men; but, in general, when the number of Union men at the ship-side is insufficient foremen do not go elsewhere to engage Union men but immediately take on non-Union men available at the ship-side. It not infrequently happens that shortages of Union men occur at particular places while Union men assembled at other places, being unaware of the opportunities of employment available, remain unemployed. There is from day to day uncertainty as to where men are likely to be required and no means are provided for bringing to the knowledge of men seeking employment the places where shortages are being experienced or for distributing the men to these places.

Following the outbreak of war in 1939 the Dock Labour (Compulsory Registration) Order 1940 resulted in a register of dock workers being drawn up in every port of commercial significance. Ernest Bevin, oft-times known as the dockers KC as a result of his brilliant advocacy before the Shaw Commission in 1919, was then Minister of Labour, and the dock workers in Aberdeen employed on handling general cargoes were quickly brought into the Scheme. Port transport work to which the Aberdeen Scheme applied covered the handling of cargo aboard ship, and between ship, quay, and transit shed. This applied throughout the larger part of the harbour with certain very important exceptions including the driving of shore cranes, metage (tallying), and the driving of certain ships cranes. Internal movement of goods was also excluded, as was delivery of goods from quay or shed, and reception of outward export cargoes on to quay or into dockside transit shed. The scheme continued to exclude prevailing practice whereby regular weekly wage workers employed by some twenty-six or more firms operating in the

115   Loading barley exports with power conveyors

harbour area handled their own goods, and the goods of others, on the quays.

The working of the wartime scheme was largely governed by the National Dock Labour Corporation Limited who initially operated from an office in Leith but later opened an office in Aberdeen. In May 1942 the National Dock Labour Corporation advised the Aberdeen Fishing Vessel Owners that the Minister of Labour had asked the Corporation to take in under the Essential Works (Dock Labour) Order, the fish porters and fish dock workers throughout the country. In due course, and after strong protest by the employers, Aberdeen fish market porters were encompassed by the Scheme, and like the general cargo dockers have been subject to the National Dock Labour Scheme ever since. It is of interest to note that a report by the Port Transit Sub-Committee written at the end of 1943 shows quite clearly that the original objectives of bringing fish market porters into the Scheme had been a failure. It had been hoped by the Ministry of Labour and the National Dock Labour Corporation that there would be completely free transferability at all times between fish market porters and commercial dockers, and this would allow porters to be used to deal with any sudden influx of commercial shipping caused by the arrrival of convoys, but the completely different working conditions and times of attendance frustrated this ideal from the very start.

At the end of the war, the Dock Workers (Regulation of Employment) Act 1946 brought together all the temporary war time schemes and applied them on a permanent nationwide basis to all ports handling significant quantities of cargo. Aberdeen was included, but many small ports which at that time were of little commercial importance continued to be excluded. Aberdeen was thus the only port north of Dundee to be subject to the legislation, and today Aberdeen and Grimsby are the only two ports in the United Kingdom where the law requires all fish to be landed by registered dock workers.

Until the next major legislation in 1967, following the report of the Committee of Inquiry headed by Lord Devlin, Aberdeen largely stayed clear

116 Unloading North Sea fish from trawlers

of the appalling trauma of industrial unrest which affected major ports throughout Britain. The major strikes in London and Liverpool in 1948 resulted in the loss of 205,000 man days, and there were further troubles in 1949 culminating in a politically inspired strike to support Canadian seamen, which resulted in 408,000 man days loss. Strikes in 1950 saw the loss in one instance of 103,000 man days, and following major troubles in London, Merseyside, the Clyde, and Manchester, and the subsequent arrest and trial at the Old Bailey of seven of a dockers strike committee, a further 230,000

117   Dockers unloading steel pipes at Waterloo Quay

118   Dockers unloading bales of woodpulp, Waterloo Quay 1973

man days were lost. In the same year some 86,000 man days were lost in another major six weeks strike, and again in 1954 a complex battle between the National Amalgamated Stevedores and Dockers Union (the 'blue union') and the Transport and General Workers Union (the 'white union') resulted in major ports losing over 700,000 man days as a result of strike action. This particular problem carried on into 1955 when a further 650,000 man days were lost, and again in 1958 333,000 man days were lost following the Smithfield strike in London.

Sometimes politically inspired, other strikes arose through conflict between Unions etc, but the fact remains that the National Dock Labour Scheme was not working satisfactorily—the dock workers tended to look to the National Dock Labour Board as being an all protecting agency for their benefit, and conversely the employers regarded the NDLB as an agency interfering between the normal relationships between employer and employee. The Board itself had no commercial responsibility for the success or otherwise of any of the ports in which it functioned. It is not surprising, therefore, that many of the smaller ports which had not handled significant quantities of cargo at the time of the 1946 Act, soon began to expand and operate profitably outwith the national scheme—two of the best known examples being Felixstowe, and Dover in England.

The Dock Work (Regulation of Employment) Act 1967 was the consequence of the Devlin Committee of Inquiry which in its turn had followed the Forster Inquiry of 1961, the Devlin Committee of 1956, the Leggett Inquiry of 1951, and other committees set up to seek ways and means of decasualising dock labour and resolving the problems of the industry. Following the enactment of the 1967 Order, and the Docks and Harbours Act 1966 which provided for the licensing of port employers, the position in Aberdeen was that the Aberdeen Fishing Vessel Owners Association were awarded the licence for employing fish market porters for the handling of wet fish, and the Aberdeen Stevedoring Company Limited became the employers for the handling of commercial cargo. This position remains unchanged at the time of writing.

119   Unloading sheep from the Northern Isles at Jamiesons Quay 1985

Critics of the Dock Labour Scheme condemn the continued existence of the National Dock Labour Board, and they argue that it serves no useful function in a modern industrial society. The disciplinary procedure makes it almost impossible for an employer to dismiss a worker except for gross misconduct such as theft, and all appeals against disciplinary action by employers have to be heard by a joint panel composed half of dock workers and half employers—this means that docker sits in judgement upon docker. The National Board located in London, remote from the outports, has the last word in determining the size of the dock labour force in any port, and is frequently out of touch with local conditions. Ports such as Aberdeen, where there is a high level of activity, have the utmost difficulty in persuading a National Board in London to allow them to recruit more labour when other major ports elsewhere, notably London, Liverpool, and the Clyde etc have a huge surplus of dock labour which can only be reduced if the men accept voluntary severance payments.

Despite these criticisms, supporters of the Scheme argue with some justification that the training of registered dock workers is second to none, that the Scheme does provide a pool of highly skilled labour, and it has the facility to introduce specialist training for the changing needs of modern cargo handling techniques. There is little doubt that with huge variations in the day to day arrivals of shipping, there has to be a proper balance struck to provide an adequate labour force, and there must be some regularity of employment guaranteed. The days of casual employment must never be allowed to return. Aberdeen is fortunate in having a highly skilled dock labour force, and productivity is high. It remains to be seen whether a future government will ever modify the present legislation, retaining for a new scheme all that is best in the National Dock Labour Scheme, removing all its worst features, and winding up the National Dock Labour Board itself having first ensured that the dock workers pension scheme is properly protected.

There is already an industry Joint Negotiating Committee to whom appeal can be made in cases of industrial dispute, and this could well be developed to control a modernised dock labour scheme. Such a scheme could then be extended to encompass all ports of commercial significance, in order to prevent any return to the evils of casual employment, and to ensure that standards of training and of skills are brought up to the same high standards as obtain in Aberdeen and other modern efficient ports.

120   Modern cargo handling, roll-on roll-off vessel mv *Astrea*, 1984

Epilogue

To the patient reader who has stayed the course thus far, a further word is merited in order to complement all that has been said of the present and of the past, and to briefly contemplate the future. Clearly this must necessarily be conjectural, but there are in fact several pointers as to what the future might hold.

In a report dated January 1984, the auditors of the European Economic Community concluded that there was already a surplus of port capacity in North East Scotland. The future of Aberdeen must, therefore, along with all other harbours from Inverness to the Forth, be affected by any major port development which might occur elsewhere within the area. A new deep water harbour located close by would thus inhibit development of all those ports, and Aberdeen would be affected more than most. The potential of North East Scotland to generate cargo is, so far as can be foreseen, strictly limited—in short the total trade of the ports hinterland cannot further be subdivided.

North Sea oil is a diminishing and finite resource. Opinions vary as to when the North Sea oil boom will pass, but since total world wide oil resources are themselves limited, the inevitable long term effect will be that world oil prices will eventually increase, and marginal fields in the North Sea will then become more financially viable. Furthermore, improved technology will allow of enhanced recovery from these and from known fields. The point in time when offshore installation traffic will cease to move into and out of Scottish harbours will likely be far into the future, although the level of activity can be expected to commence its decline—albeit ever so slowly—within the next few years.

With a reduction, and an eventual complete demise of offshore installation traffic through Aberdeen Harbour, greater dependence upon the older traditional trades will resume. Agriculture and fishing are renewable resources, and they can thus expect to be figuring in harbour traffic statistics throughout the foreseeable future. In due course it is to be hoped that worthwhile exports of offshore equipment will be handled—always providing manufacturing industry can take advantage of the opportunities now presented locally. Worldwide offshore markets will, however, not demand goods in large volumes, but in relatively small quantities in terms or tonnage, and the harbour impact is therefore not likely to be enormous.

He would be a wise man who could foretell what other new traffic will develop, what new industries will become established in North East Scotland, or what new importation requirement will be imposed by the social demands of the twenty-first century community, their life style, and their living and eating habits. Man must eat to live, and some specialist foodstuffs will probably continue to be imported, or produced in areas south of the border. A world demand for grain, and a continuing fishing industry must

121 Cruise liner mv *Istra* at International Passenger Terminal, Atlantic Wharf

necessarily ensure a continuing need to handle fish, grain, and fertilisers in the harbour. Dependent upon some rearrangement of world economics, North East Scottish farmers could well become major suppliers of foodstuff to third world countries unable to support themselves. Aberdeen Harbour has deep water, and could well be a major exporting harbour for food and cereals destined to less fortunate regions such as East Africa.

Future change in cargo handling technology is also certain to influence future development of the harbour. High labour costs have already, on a world wide basis, given impetus to high technology methods, and in the last two decades the emergence of roll-on/roll-off traffic in the short sea, and even in the long distance, trades has been a most significant factor affecting all British ports. Similarly the change toward unitisation of cargo on pallets has evolved into the use of international shipping containers now also used on trade routes worldwide. The further decline in manual handling of goods can be confidently predicted, albeit at a slower pace, and it can also be confidently predicted that there will be improvements in technology for the handling of bulk materials. The trend toward larger ships can only go so far, especially in the short sea trades, and thus the erosion of traffic by ports capable of handling the largest size of vessels seems unlikely to have much further impact on traffic.

In the long term there is likely to be development of improved bulk handling facilities—perhaps using pneumatic handling techniques or more flexible variations of bucket elevators. The use of sophisticated "kangaroo" grabbing cranes with built in hoppers are also likely to figure in future development and crane replacement programmes. New ferry services can also be expected to appear based on the roll-on/roll-off concept. Aberdeen Harbour Board played an important role in a recent investigation as to the viability of a coastal ro-ro service, and whilst the project was not found viable at the present time, eventually, an increase in world oil prices may very well make the cost of movement of goods by sea cheaper than by road or rail. Coastal ferry services could thus possibly be developed in the long term future, and there is already sufficient cargo generated in North East Scotland to justify a ferry from Aberdeen to Continental Europe. The opening of a channel tunnel may have some effect on Aberdeen, but this is likely to be minimal.

Tourism is also a major growth area, with a potential for many more cruise ships to call in Aberdeen—where else can passenger liners be moored so close to the heart of a city, or so close to so much magnificent scenery? A more sophisticated development of the leisure scene could well justify regular passenger ferry services from the vast market place of Europe to Aberdeen

Harbour which is ideally placed for the main tourist zones of Royal Deeside, and the Highlands.

If ever commercial traffic were to decline significantly along with the corresponding decline in offshore installation traffic, overall harbour activity might easily decline to a level which would make it expedient for the harbour to develop more into other areas of the leisure market. The north east coast of Scotland is not well suited to leisure sailing, but there does exist a small potential, and therefore if space is vacated by commercial shipping, this could then be used by pleasure craft for which there is no provision at present.

Sound husbandry of resources, careful fiscal policies, and recent replacement of all facilities allows Aberdeen Harbour to face the future with more confidence than most ports. If the entrance channel is widened and deepened, larger vessels can be handled within certain constraints. Thus, provided high levels of service can be continued and improved upon, Aberdeen Harbour should have sufficient funds to continue developing facilities in accordance with changes in technology. The harbour will undoubtedly continue to be the major port on the coast for North East Scotland throughout the next century—always providing there are no significant port developments elsewhere.

These then are the ways in which harbour traffic might possibly develop in the future. Drawing to a close, the author is conscious of the many human stories left untold in this book, the bitter strife of the nineteenth century would itself take two volumes of similar size to fully describe, and inevitably the critics will point to many other errors of omission. It may be that time will improve historical knowledge, and new facts may be uncovered by future generations, and by other researchers. The story is, however, one of immense interest. It is a tale of remarkable human endeavour, of enormous foresight and clever planning, and above all it is a story which reflects the greatest credit upon those who have given of their life's work to the harbour. Inevitably the names of great engineers, of great managers, and of great Board members and Harbour Commissioners, predominate in a story such as this. These people would, however, be as nothing without the humblest of labour, and any modest success which has been achieved by Aberdeen Harbour is in no small part due to those legions of wonderful men and women who, now lost in anonimity, have made Aberdeen the foremost harbour in the North of Scotland.

facing page
122 Aberdeen Harbour, aerial view 1984

Appendix 1

FIRST REPORT

BY

JOHN SMEATON, Engineer,

UPON

THE HARBOUR

OF

THE CITY OF ABERDEEN

19th FEBRUARY, 1770

The principal complaint attending this Harbour is, the difficulty of entry, occasioned by a Bar a little without the Harbour mouth; and a shifting bed of sand, gravel, and shingle, on the north side of the entry; which, by the action of the seas, when the wind is in the north-easterly quarter, drives into the main channel, choking it up in different degrees; according to the degree of violence of the sea, the state of the tides, and of the land-speats, floods, or freshes in the river Dee, which here falls into the sea.

When I was there, which was in the month of August, 1769, the entry was then said to be in a good state; and on sounding it upon the 7th of that month, which was the sixth day after the new moon (and consequently the tides in a mean state, between spring and neap), I found full four feet of water upon the Bar at low water, and at high water the same day full fourteen feet; but, it is said that the ordinary spring tides make much about the same depth upon the Bar at high water, and that at low water the Bar is left with only the run of the river over it. The neap tides, it is said, usually make ten feet water upon the Bar; but this is to be understood (I suppose) at such times as the entry is in a good state.

On sounding at low water, I found the body of the Bar to be composed of loose stones, of different sizes, and the whole intermixed and compacted together with gravel; over which was a layer of sand from six inches to a foot in thickness, which, after great land freshes is said to be quite swept away, and the stones and gravel left bare, which is its best state. The Bar is but of short extent, and both within and without we quickly get more water by three feet.

Without the Bar the water gradually deepens, and forms a very good road for ships to ride at low water, and is naturally protected from all winds except the north-easterly and easterly, which blow right into the Harbour's mouth; so that, was there a little more depth of water over the Bar, and this *certain*, this Harbour would be capable of affording very good protection to merchant ships trading into those seas.

The cause of the annoyance of the Harbour's mouth appears to me to be this:— The whole Coast, which stretches away northerly, is apparently for miles a flat and sandy shore; and, I suppose, from the Harbour of Aberdeen till it meets with the point of Buchan-ness, which is at the distance of seven leagues, continues of the same kind; consequently the wind at N.E. acting obliquely upon it, brings the sand and gravel therewith intermixed coastwise towards the south, and, as the Coast from the south side of the entry of this Harbour stretches away nearly east for about three-fourths of a mile, those sands would naturally be deposited in the angle of the Coast formed at the Harbour's mouth, did not the necessity of the land waters of the river Dee, in finding a passage to sea, force themselves a vent; and which they maintain more or less clear, according as the circumstance of winds, tides, and freshes, balance one against another.

A hard gale of wind at north-east, as already mentioned, gradually brings the sands and gravel coastwise southward, and puts in agitation that already lodged in the bank on the north side of the Harbour's mouth, at the same time forcing it into the entry; and, if at that time it happens to be spring tide, and little fresh water in the river, a strong tide of flood being the consequence, greatly co-operates with the wind and seas in carrying a great quantity of sand and gravel into the channel of the river; and the fresh water in the river being supposed then very short, the reflux will be very languid; and being counteracted by the impetus of the sea, it cannot return: and a continuance of weather and circumstances of this kind will put the mouth of the Harbour into the worst state, in which it must necessarily remain, till, by a contrary disposition of circumstances, a contrary effect is produced.

On the other hand, a continuance of great land floods, either at spring or neap tides, accompanied either with offshore winds, or moderate ones at N.E., gives the greatest advantage in scouring out the sands and gravel from about the Harbour's mouth; carrying it out into the road, from whence, by degrees, it gets round the point of Girdleness. And if, towards the close of the work, there happens along with a strong land fresh, low spring ebbs, which gives the current the greatest fall to sea, and at the same time runs bare over the Bar, with a moderate wind at N.E. which will give the sand some agitation without much impetus,—under these circumstances, the stony body of the Bar will be run clear of the sand, and the Harbour's mouth will be put into its best state, and so will remain, till the contrary causes produce, as before, the contrary effects. And, in this state of fluctuation must the entry of the Harbour of Aberdeen ever remain, till something is done to counteract the effects of that arrangement of circumstances, whose natural tendency is to do harm.

The *only means* by which I can see this is likely to be effected, is by the erection of a North Pier, which will directly tend to the cure of the evil complained of; for it will not only keep the land freshes more confined in a body till they come into deeper water; but, what is of more consequence, it will in a great measure prevent the sand and gravel from being driven in. It will not, indeed, stop the continual driving of the matter coastwise from the north; but, after the back or outside of the Pier is filled up with sand, &c. to a certain degree, it will then go round the Pier-head; and by the superior action of middling freshes and spring ebbs, will be kept in deeper water, and so get round the point of Girdleness without first getting into the Harbour's mouth; or, at least, not to that degree as to obstruct the navigation in and out. By this means as the bar will not only be kept clear down to the stone bed; but by lifting the larger sort of stones by art, the remaining gravel will wash out into deeper water, so as to make, as it may reasonably be expected, full two feet more water than there is now in its best state.

I can see no objection to the putting this work into immediate execution, save the expense of it. To reduce this as much as possible, I have endeavoured to propose such a construction, as, consistent with that solidity and permanency that a work of this kind ought to have, consists of the smallest quantity of materials and workmanship that I can think fit; and, as the materials which nature furnishes here are of the best kind for the purpose, and arise near the place, I am in hopes that they will be raised and put together considerably cheaper than I have supposed in my estimate; which, for that reason, I desire may be considered in no other light, than a form or blank, comprehending species and quantities,—for as my stay in Aberdeen was obliged to be so short, the necessary examinations immediately relating to the Harbour, prevented my entering into those inquiries which tended only to acquaint myself with the price and value of labour and materials.

I, therefore, can only fill up the blanks, by comparison with what has been done at other places less advantageously situated with respect to materials, and perhaps that of labour also;—in order, therefore, to come at a real estimate suited to the place, I must beg leave to refer myself to the inquiries of the Magistrates concerning prices, or to a Committee deputed by them for that purpose; and which, from their particular knowledge of the country and of the workmen, will, I apprehend, be done to more advantage than I could have done myself, without a longer stay than my other avocations could possibly admit of.

One thing, however, I must beg leave to suggest, that though what I now offer is, as I apprehend, the complete thing, which I expect to answer in the best manner; yet, I am of opinion, it will be found, if the Pier is not carried out so far by two hundred feet, that it will in a great measure relieve the present annoyances; nay, that it will be of singular service, if carried out but just beyond the present Pier, on the south side of the entry, in which case it will be shortened by three hundred and fifty feet. In the former case, the expense will be reduced according to my estimate by £2028, and in the latter by £3549; and as the work ought to be begun from Sandness point, where it is easiest and cheapest to be done; by this means the workmen will gradually learn the way of doing it to the best advantage, and will probably be able to contract for the more expensive part, upon better terms, than would seem to them feasible at the beginning; and, as the work advances, the benefit and effect will be seen, so that it need not to be carried further out, than by experience shall be proved necessary.

I come now to the improvements that may be made in the internal part of the Harbour, and here I cannot but lament that the course of the river is distracted by so many channels, and covers so great a breadth of ground at high water; which want of confinement is not only detrimental to the procuring of a deep channel at the Harbour's mouth, but within the Harbour also; and it is particularly disadvantageous, that the main current of the river does not sweep the face of the Town's Quay:—This I should without any hesitation advise to be done by art, was it not for the fishing properties upon the main channel; but, as I must suppose them irrevocably established, it remains to point out what is the best that can now be done, the fishings remaining as they are. I observe that, within the point of Sandness, there is near the same water as over the Bar, till the main river channel and navigation-channel divide, which part of the river is marked in the Plan, as the *Stell Fishing*. In this part of the river, which is land-locked from all winds, vessels that will bear the ground, and whose draught of water is such as not to go further up, may safely deliver their cargoes, or shelter themselves when they come in by way of refuge; but, after the aforesaid division, the navigation-channel becomes immediately shallow, carrying however ten feet water till we arrive above the New Pier; when opposite the Ropery and Dock-yard, it falls a little shallower to nine feet four inches; from thence it holds nine feet and a half to ten feet, till meeting with the Town's Pier or Quay, it again breaks into two channels, viz. that which stretches along the face of the Pier, and that which is called the Blacky Pool. The navigation-channel by the Pier side, from the aforesaid division, falls off at first to nine, then to eight, and gradually to seven feet water.

The desirable improvement pointed out to me, and which seems of great consequence to the trade of the city, is to deepen the navigation-channel, quite away from the New Pier to the west-end of the Town's Pier or Quay.

I observed, when there, that little or none of the current water of the river Dee, in its common state at low water, goes down either the channel by the face of the Pier or the Blacky Pool; all the outlets from the main stream that might be likely to take this course, being barricaded by stone dykes, raised from two to three feet, or thereabouts, above the ordinary surface of the Dee's water; so that nothing worth notice, till the water is swelled above those dykes, can go down the above mentioned channels, save the water of two small burns which empty themselves by the navigation-channel. With these helps, however, but principally by the currency that passes through it and the Blacky Pool, in time of such speats as overflow the aforesaid dykes, the navigation-channel is kept open.

It has been proposed to bank in the low grounds lying west of the Old Pier, so as to pen in the spring tides, and at that place to erect a sluice to be drawn at low water; and by making an artificial scour to deepen the aforesaid navigation-channel.

Great effects are capable of being produced by the operation and judicious management of sluices, in situations adapated thereto; that is, where there is a great command of fresh water, or a considerable declivity in the part to be scoured. Here, the water to be pent in must be in a great measure tide water, which, as the embankation would in a great degree prevent all currency through it, would be subject to fill up the reservoir. And as the water would not be considerable in itself, and the length according to the navigation-channel near a mile, upon four feet only of descent at low water; I fear, these circumstances considered, the effect would not be found answerable to expectation. On the other hand, the embankation, preventing the speats which overflow the dykes from getting in at the head of the navigation-channel, the principal natural agent would be prevented from operating, and which I should be sorry to lose. Was the long dyke, called in the Plan the *little* dyke, broke down and removed, I make no doubt but that, in the course of a few years, the main stream of the river Dee would make its passage by way of the Denburn into the navigation-channel, and, by degrees of itself, produce the effect desired, and with a little help, would do it in a very few years. I state this, not upon any supposition that the little dyke is likely to be removed, but more strongly to show the use of such natural advantages as still remain. I do not suppose, however, that any use that can be made of the remaining advantages will, of themselves, greatly deepen the navigation-channel; but this I suppose, that, after it is made deeper by art, those natural advantages may be so applied as to keep it equally clean at a greater depth as they now do at a lesser.

The whole channel, from the New Pier to the Town's Pier, does not need a great deal to make it full ten feet water; and it may be very successfully deepened by a ballast lighter, constructed like those used upon the river Thames for getting ballast for the ships. Those lighters work by direction of the Trinity-House, upon such shoals as are most obnoxious to the navigation of that river; and all the ships of that port are obliged to take their ballast from them at a certain price. Perhaps much ballast is not taken out from the port of Aberdeen; but such as is may be supplied by the lighter, in aid, as far as it goes, of the expense of raising it.

The channel for the whole length of the Pier or Quay I would propose to be deepened by the mattock and spade, at low water; which deepening, being done two feet at a mean, will give ten feet water to the middle of the Pier, where now there is but seven feet six inches; and this being done to a breadth of sixty feet, will admit of two vessels to lie abreast with sufficient passage. This work will be attended with no extraordinary expense in proportion to the utility thereof, and which will endure several years before the state of the channel will return to what it now is; yet it would undoubtedly return by degrees to the same state, unless some counter-balance be applied to prevent it. What I would therefore recommend for this purpose is as follows:—

To erect a strong stone dyke, beginning at the head of the Inch-dyke, in the direction of the single dotted line, to the beacon upon the Trinity Inch; or, if it should anywise happen to interfere with the raik fishing, to carry it from a lower part of the Inch-dyke to the said beacon, according to the direction of the double dotted line. This dyke to be made so as to rise above, and keep in, the water of the high land floods, at half ebb of the tide, and to be made firm, so that the current may in great land floods at high water go over it, without hurting it. By this means, the greatest part of the water, that in time of speats flows over the present dykes, and making its way partly by the Blacky Pool, partly over the surface of the higher lands, and partly by the navigation-channel, along the face of the Pier, will all be constrained to go through the channel alongside the Pier, altogether; and therefore will be as well enabled to keep clear that channel at ten feet deep, as the present channel joined to Blacky Pool is to keep it at that mean depth, from their junction to the junction of the main river at the stell fishing. As these operations are plain and simple, and will be attended with no considerable expense, I earnestly recommend their execution.

It is also very practicable in like manner to join the Old Pier, by a dyke across the Trinity Inch, to the elbow of the river, a little above the Inch-dyke, according to the single dotted line A B; and also, by putting Sluices upon the opening between the north-end of the Old Pier and the west-end of the Town's Pier or Quay, to pen in the tides, in order to make artificial scours; but, as the building and maintenance of sluices would be expensive, if made so capacious as not to be an impediment to the current and action of the land flood waters, as above mentioned, and would have no considerable effect, unless the water was pent up higher than the present fishing dykes (the banks whereof, if so, would, in a great measure, prevent the flood waters going that way), it therefore appears, that since sluices of any kind are likely to prevent more good than they will do, that the plain, natural, and simple method first described, of making a dyke according to the single dotted line first mentioned, is the most eligible to be put in execution. Upon the whole, I am of opinion the methods pointed out to be pursued, without and within, will remedy the complaints the Harbour is subject to, as far as is above specified, and possibly in a still greater degree.

J. SMEATON

Austhorpe, 9th February, 1770

Appendix 2

ACTS OF PARLIAMENT

Although all ports and harbours are subject to a wide range of national legislation, most ports are set up under their own specific Acts of Parliament, and few have for so long been the subject of their own legislation as Aberdeen Harbour. The Harbour is also specifically mentioned in Royal Charters granted by King David I and King Malcolm IV in favour of the Bishops of Aberdeen, and in the Royal Charters subsequently granted to the City. The ensuing legislation is, however, specific to the Harbour.

1641 Charles I

An Act by the Scottish Parliament on 17 November 1641, confirming a Charter by King Charles I in favour of the City of Aberdeen, dated 9th September 1638, which in turn confirms several previous Charters in favour of the Royal Burgh granted by King James VI and earlier Scottish Kings and many of which includes references to the Harbour.

1682 Charles II

An Act made on the 7 July 1682 in Edinburgh authorising a general collection to be taken up at parish churches throughout Scotland, and the monies to be collected and paid to the Treasurer of the City of Aberdeen for harbour construction and repairs.

1773 George III c.29

'An Act for deepening, cleansing, and making more commodious, the Harbour of Aberdeen; for erecting new Piers and Quays therein; and for regulating Ships and Vessels trading into, and out of, the said Harbour. 1st April 1773.'

The first section of the North Pier was built by Smeaton under this Act—the first significant improvement to the mediaeval harbour.

1795 George III c.41

'An Act to continue the Term, and alter and enlarge the Powers, of an Act, made in the Thirteenth Year of the Reign of His present Majesty, intituled an Act for deepening, cleansing, and making more commodious the Harbour of Aberdeen: for erecting New Piers and Quays therein; and for regulating Ships and Vessels trading into and going out of, the said harbour. 28th April 1795.'

For further improvements and powers to raise more money to pay for the new works.

1796 George II c.68

'An Act for making and maintaining a Navigable Canal from the Harbour of Aberdeen, in the Parish of Aberdeen or Saint Nicholas, into the River Don, at or near the South end of the Bridge over the same (adjacent to the Royal Burgh of Inverurie), in the Parish of Kintore, all within the County of Aberdeen, North Britain. 26th April 1796.'

1797 George III c.101

'An Act for enlarging and improving the Harbour of Aberdeen, for building new Quays, Wharfs, and Docks, and for making new Roads and Passages, and widening others leading to and from the said harbour. 4th July 1797.'

1810 George III c.70

'An Act to amend several Acts of the Thirteenth, Thirty-fifth and Thirty-seventh Years of His present Majesty for deepening and making more commodious the Harbour of Aberdeen. 18th May 1810.'

This important Act authorised extensions of the North Pier, and extensive harbour improvements by Telford. Improved regulation and power to increase charges were authorised.

1813 George III c.157

'An Act for further improving the Harbour of Aberdeen. 22nd June 1813.'

Provision for appropriation of lands belonging to the City and arrangements for purchase thereof. Also compensation for loss at certain salmon fishings and provision for extenstion of fishings. Amendment to powers of the Trustees, and arrangements for election of auditors.

1829 George IV c.34

'An Act for the Improvement of the Harbour of Aberdeen. 14th May 1829.'

Provision made for a new constitution including the election of five Burgess of Guild and one member of the Incorporated Trades. Further improvements and powers to borrow money, raise charges, appoint auditors, and re-arrange certain salmon fishings authorised.

1843 Victoria c.72

'An Act for Improving and Maintaining the Harbour of Aberdeen. 12th July 1843.'

Revision of constitution with nine Burgesses of Guild and three members of Incorporated Trades. Further harbour extension and improvements authorised including construction of a wet dock, with new rates and charges to pay for improvement. A very comprehensive Act with extensive regulatory provisions.

1847 Victoria c.39

'An Act to authorise the Purchase by the Aberdeen Railway Company of a Piece of Ground at the upper Part of the Inches and upper Part of the Harbour of Aberdeen now vested in the Aberdeen Harbour Commissioners, and to enable such Commissioners to make certain Alterations and new Works connected with such Harbour. 21st June 1847.'

Power granted to Commissioners to sell ground to the Railway Company, and revenue therefrom to be applied to harbour works. Provision for new harbour works, regulation for laying down of timber, and clarification as to disposal of rates from pilotage, metage, weighing etc.

1868 Victoria c.138

'An Act for improving and maintaining the Harbour of Aberdeen. 13th July 1868.'

Constitution further amended to provide for 12 elected commissioners, the Lord Provost and six Baillies together with the Dean of Guild and eleven councillors. Provision also made for further extension of the North Pier, construction of the South Breakwater, diversion of the River Dee, and further harbour improvement. Harbour Regulations were revised, and increased charges authorised to offset debts and pay for new works.

1871 Victoria c.98
'An Act to confer further Powers on the Aberdeen Harbour Commissioners. 13th July 1871.'

Provision for purchase of salmon fishings together with extended powers to borrow money for this purpose.

1879 Victoria c.88
'An Act to confer further Powers on the Aberdeen Harbour Commissioners. 3rd July 1879.'

Authority to review rates and dues leviable, and to increase the Commissioners borrowing power.

1887 Piers and Harbour Orders Confirmation (No 1) Act
'An Act to confirm certain Provisional Orders made by the Board of Trade under the General Pier and Harbour Act, 1861, relating to Aberdeen, Alum Bay, Greenock, Sandown, and Teignmouth. 5th July 1887.'

An act confirming an Order amending the 1879 Act, and for conferring further powers on the Commissioners to apply new rates on goods and vessels, and to set aside quays for landing of fish.

1895 Aberdeen Harbour Act
'An Act to amend and consolidate the Acts relating to the Harbour of Aberdeen; and for other purposes. 6th July 1895.'

A comprehensive Act repealing previous legislation, re-affirming the constitution, providing for increased borrowing powers, increases in charges, extended powers to improve, maintain, administer, and regulate the harbour. The powers of improvement facilitated construction of Albert Basin, improvements to Victoria Dock entrance, construction of Jamieson's Quay etc.

1899 Aberdeen Harbour Act
'To confer further powers under the Aberdeen Harbour Commissioners. 6th June 1899.'

Increased borrowing powers to carry out works authorised by the 1895 Act.

1907 Aberdeen Harbour Order Confirmation Act
'To confirm a Provisional Order under the Private Legislation Procedure (Scotland) Act 1899 relating to Aberdeen Harbour. 28th August 1907.'

Increased powers of Commissioners to borrow money, regulation as to the application of monies borrowed, and amended priorities of bonds.

1909 Aberdeen Harbour Order Confirmation Act
'An Act to confirm a Provisional Order under the Private Legislation Procedure (Scotland) Act 1899 relating to Aberdeen Harbour. 20th September 1909.'

Further powers conferred on the Harbour Commissioners to acquire land for harbour construction, to increase rates and charges, and to modify qualifications for harbour electors.

1920 Aberdeen Harbour Order Confirmation Act
'An Act to confirm a Provisional Order under the Private Legislation Procedure (Scotland) Act 1899 relating to Aberdeen Harbour. 3rd December 1920.'

Extension of the Harbour Acts to 1935, and to require copies of Annual Accounts to be sent to the Ministry of Transport.

1921 Pilotage Orders Confirmation (No 7) Act
The Aberdeen Pilotage Order 1921

An Order under the Pilotage Act 1913, in which the Aberdeen pilotage district is defined and certain provisions made as to pilotage which is thereafter to be compulsory.

1924 The Aberdeen Pilotage Order

Modifying the limits of the pilotage district. 26 May 1924.

1924 Aberdeen Harbour Order Confirmation Act

'To confirm a Provisional Order under the Private Legislation Procedure (Scotland) Act 1899 relating to Aberdeen Harbour. 21st February 1924.'

Increased borrowing powers, and regulations as to application. Amended priority of Bonds.

1924 Aberdeen Harbour (Rates) Order Confirmation Act

'To confirm the Provisional Order under the Private Legislation Procedure (Scotland) Act 1899 relating to Aberdeen Harbour. 18th December 1924.'

To make provision as to the statutory maximum rates, dues, tolls and charges leviable at the Harbour of Aberdeen.

1932 Aberdeen Harbour Order Confirmation Act

'An Act to confirm a Provisional Order under the Private Legislation Procedure (Scotland) Act 1899 relating to Aberdeen Harbour. 15th November 1932.'

Extension of Harbour Acts to 1949, new powers of wreck removal.

1933 Aberdeen Harbour (Rates) Order Confirmation Act

'An Act to confirm a Provisional Order under the Private Legislation (Scotland) Act 1899 relating to Aberdeen Harbour (Rates). 28th July 1933.'

Provision for revised Rates for vessels, and goods. Rates for seaplanes and floating docks etc introduced.

1939 Aberdeen Harbour (Superannuation) Order Confirmation Act

'An Act to confirm a Provisional Order under the Private Legislation Procedure (Scotland) Act 1936 relating to Aberdeen Harbour (Superannuation). 4th August 1939.'

An order authorising the Commissioners to establish a staff superannuation scheme.

1946 Aberdeen Harbour Order Confirmation Act

'An Act to Confirm a Provisional Order under the Private Legislation Procedure (Scotland) Act 1936 relating to Aberdeen Harbour. 6th November 1946.'

Extension of Harbour Acts to remain in force until 1952.

1949 Aberdeen Harbour Order Confirmation Act

'An Act to Confirm a Provisional Order under the Private Legislation Procedure (Scotland) Act 1936 relating to Aberdeen Harbour. 24th November 1949.'

Extension of Harbour Acts to remain in force until 1956.

1950 Aberdeen Harbour Order Confirmation Act

'An Act to Confirm a Provisional Order under the Private Legislation Procedure (Scotland) Act 1936 relating to Aberdeen Harbour. 12th July 1950.'

Confirming an Order with regard to the rates leviable by the Commissioners, and to authorise further borrowing powers for harbour improvements.

1953 Aberdeen Harbour Confirmation Act
'To Confirm a Provisional Order under the Private Legislation Procedure (Scotland) Act 1936 relating to Aberdeen Harbour. 6th May 1953.'

Extension of Harbour Acts to remain in force until 1959.

1956 Aberdeen Harbour Order Confirmation Act
'An Act to confirm a Provisional Order under the Private Legislation Procedure (Scotland) Act 1936 relating to Aberdeen Harbour. 2nd August 1956.'

Amendment of the 1953 Act to allow Harbours acts 1895–1953 to remain in force until 1959.

1960 Aberdeen Harbour Order Confirmation Act
'An Act to Confirm a Provisional Order under the Private Legislation Procedure (Scotland) Act 1936 relating to Aberdeen Harbour. 20th December 1960.'

This the primary legislation under which the modern Port and Harbour operates. It provides for the incorporation of the Aberdeen Harbour Board and the transfer to and vesting therein of the harbour undertaking of the former Aberdeen Harbour Commissioners, and determines and regulates the administration of the port and harbour and provides for other purposes connected therewith.

1968 The Aberdeen Harbour Revision Order
Amends the 1960 Act by allowing the Board to effect a change in the financial year, and also provides for Board members communications to be sent to their place of business.

1969 Aberdeen Corporation (Fish Market) Order Confirmation Act
'An Act to confirm a Provisional Order under the Private Legislation Procedure (Scotland) Act 1936, relating to the Aberdeen Corporation (Fish Market). 25th June 1969.'

Provision for the transfer of the fish market formerly belonging to the Corporation of the City of Aberdeen to the Aberdeen Harbour Board, and to confer powers on the Board with respect to the regulation of the fish market, raising of charges and making of byelaws etc. The sum of £37,500 is specified as being payable by the Harbour Board to the Common Good Fund of the City.

1971 Aberdeen Harbour Revision Order
Amends the 1960 Act by increasing the Board's borrowing powers from £150,000 to £300,000 by overdraft for capital purposes. Borrowing powers for current expenditure were also increased from £100,000 to £200,000.

1972 Aberdeen Harbour Revision Order
Further increases in the Board's power to borrow money.

1972 Aberdeen Harbour Revision Order
Further increase in borrowing powers from £2 million to £4 million for capital purposes.

1972 Aberdeen Harbour Order Confirmation Act
'An Act to confirm a Provisional Order under the Private Legislation Procedure (Scotland) Act1936, relating to Aberdeen Harbour. 13th November 1972.'

Powers to make and operate schemes for regulating the berthing of fishing vessels in the fish market and for other purposes connected therewith.

1973 The Dock and Harbour Act 1966 (Commencement No 12 Order)

An Order to bring into operation Section 1 of the Docks and Harbours Act 1966 in the port of Aberdeen. In essence this appoints Aberdeen Harbour Board as the licensing authority for Dock Labour in the port.

1974 Aberdeen Harbour Revision Order

An order to empower the Board to make arrangements with an insurance company for the provision of pensions and benefits.

1976 Aberdeen Harbour Revision Order

Powers to increase borrowing powers for capital works from £4 million to £6 million.

1984 Aberdeen Harbour Revision Order

Amending the 1960 Act so as to authorise the Board to increase the amount of rates to be paid by a person in order to qualify as an elector, to increase the cost of boatmen's licences, and the amount of its rewards for meritorious service by the staff.

Miscellaneous

Aberdeen Harbour, in common with all other British ports and harbours, is also affected by a great deal of national legislation, much of which is specific to docks and harbours. Most important amongst these are the undernoted:

> Harbours, Docks and Piers Clauses Act 1847
> The Merchant Shipping Acts 1894 and 1906
> The Docks Regulations, 1934
>   (Made under Section 79 of the Factory and Workshop Act, 1901)
> The Dock Workers (Regulation of Employment) Act 1946
> Harbours Act 1964
> Docks and Harbours Act 1966
> Dock Workers (Regulation of Employment)(Amendment) Order 1967
> Dock Work Regulation Act 1976
> Merchant Shipping Act 1979
> Pilotage Act 1983

Aberdeen Harbour has also been affected over the years by legislation promoted by other bodies. Notable among these are Acts of 1796 and 1801 and 1810 for the construction and completion of the Aberdeenshire Canal Navigation from the harbour to Inverurie. Several City Acts including the Aberdeen Extension and Improvement Act, 1883, the Aberdeen Corporation Water Act, 1885, the Aberdeen Corporation Act, 1891, and the Aberdeen Corporation Act, 1899, all affected the harbour. Likewise, several Railway Acts relate to the construction, maintenance, and use of lines of rails on the quays of the harbour, and these include the Great North of Scotland Railway Amendment Act, 1854, the Great North of Scotland Railway Consolidation Act, 1859, the Great North of Scotland Railway Act, 1881, the Caledonian Railway (Further Powers) Act, 1882, the Caledonian Railway Act, 1887, the Aberdeen Joint Passenger Station Act, 1889, and others.

Appendix 3

STATISTICS

STATEMENT showing Register Tonnage of Vessels (exclusive of Fishing Vessels) entering Harbour, and Quantity of Goods imported and exported in each year, from 1 October 1881.

Year ending 30 September	Tonnage of Vessels		Goods	
	Coastwise	Foreign	Imported	Exported
	Tons.	Tons.	Tons.	Tons.
1882	504,503	82,670	522,544	167,524
1883	526,211	83,198	558,795	164,434
1884	563,863	102,674	612,414	168,453
1885	561,222	101,275	582,630	150,622
1886	569,312	95,792	620,367	156,907
1887	580,356	90,203	619,764	173,293
1888	593,163	116,431	681,634	165,483
1889	560,650	120,535	723,525	151,331
1890	603,599	144,250	710,308	161,638
1891	625,874	160,753	734,944	177,508
1892	630,507	163,760	778,715	166,775
1893	657,782	130,073	767,741	163,191
1894	686,613	157,776	840,747	170,040
1895	735,126	149,159	888,577	172,319
1896	771,056	147,884	907,808	185,382
1897	811,739	160,404	958,857	188,452
1898	800,584	168,321	1,006,936	189,011
1899	798,189	158,397	1,003,740	199,721
1900	782,380	163,538	1,022,850	203,411
1901	785,907	187,905	1,046,984	204,597

Note: During the year ending 30 September 1901 the numbers of Animals imported and exported were as follows:

	Cattle	Sheep	Pigs
Imported	7,320	27,932	1,207
Exported	2,536	36,833	6,567

STATEMENT showing the Number of Arrivals of White Fishing Vessels and Quantity of Fish landed in each year, from 1 October 1887.

Year ending 30 September	Trawl Fishing Vessels	Steam Line Vessels	Sail Line Vessels	Fish Landed
				Cwts.
1888	2,763	296	7,751	133,180
1889	3,117	605	6,570	161,300
1890	3,389	958	9,793	230,320
1891	3,714	925	11,522	287,100
1892	3,764	1,537	11,705	332,240
1893	4,316	1,688	11,385	399,840
1894	4,049	1,783	10,522	403,240
1895	5,024	1,693	11,484	532,780
1896	4,873	2,215	11,832	532,200
1897	5,957	2,529	10,123	599,520
1898	6,473	2,424	9,868	712,660
1899	7,455	2,046	10,412	836,560
1900	7,575	1,941	8,357	911,260
1901	8,044	1,762	8,155	1,091,660

STATEMENT showing Register Tonnage of Vessels (exclusive of Fishing Vessels) entering Harbour, and Quantity of Goods imported and exported in each year, from 1 October, 1900

Year ended 30 Sept.	Tonnage of Vessels			Goods		
	Coastwise†	Foreign	Total†	Imported	Exported*	Total*
	Tons.	Tons.	Tons.	Tons.	Tons.	Tons.
1901	785,907	187,905	973,812	1,046,984	204,597	1,251,581
1902	808,966	170,644	979,610	1,091,002	209,686	1,300,688
1903	831,830	165,296	997,126	1,100,817	214,009	1,314,826
1904	806,396	184,299	990,695	1,112,686	194,593	1,307,279
1905	799,144	179,087	978,231	1,103,989	202,605	1,306,594
1906	813,716	180,656	994,372	1,126,331	224,787	1,351,118
1907	827,074	182,556	1,009,630	1,171,467	197,185	1,368,652
1908	825,703	201,275	1,026,978	1,200,681	206,753	1,407,434
1909	836,327	190,163	1,026,490	1,165,060	210,554	1,375,614
1910	839,537	190,250	1,029,787	1,206,331	213,026	1,419,357
1911	840,290	180,723	1,021,013	1,205,754	209,957	1,415,711
1912	830,818	184,707	1,015,525	1,223,859	216,753	1,440,612
1913	887,829	180,210	1,068,039	1,273,509	209,642	1,483,151
1914	834,294	174,670	1,008,964	1,222,173	205,642	1,427,815
1915	585,574	82,502	668,076	805,042	143,123	948,165
1916	419,723	92,891	512,614	646,376	116,295	762,671
1917	260,008	33,506	293,514	355,386	90,344	445,730

STATEMENT showing Register Tonnage of Vessels (exclusive of Fishing Vessels) entering Harbour, and Quantity of Goods imported and exported in each year, from 1 October, 1900 (Continued)

Year ended 30 Sept.	Tonnage of Vessels			Goods		
	Coastwise†	Foreign	Total†	Imported	Exported*	Total*
1918	183,347	28,674	212,021	194,495	60,047	254,542
1919	257,768	62,173	319,941	364,936	66,055	430,991
1920	442,520	100,751	543,271	762,302	93,751	856,053
1921	384,359	122,678	507,037	585,363	103,214	688,577
1922	494,264	140,049	634,313	741,956	130,115	872,071
1923	505,001	201,926	706,927	726,481	138,721	865,202
1924	556,467	259,539	816,006	906,047	152,488	1,058,535
1925	586,836	279,527	866,363	970,991	152,752	1,123,743
1926	521,323	326,223	847,546	952,264	157,627	1,109,891
1927	556,704	309,309	866,013	955,007	170,917	1,125,924
1928	614,462	290,825	905,287	1,005,779	143,305	1,149,084
1929	661,692	276,739	938,431	1,057,848	157,050	1,214,898
1930	667,974	297,061	965,035	1,060,532	146,643	1,207,175
1931	684,900	247,066	931,966	1,207,831	119,147	1,146,978
1932	669,872	297,382	967,254	970,258	115,177	1,085,435
1933	673,245	270,243	943,488	941,212	136,437	1,077,649
1934	649,792	283,299	933,091	916,306	341,999	1,258,305
1935	678,926	273,127	952,053	974,869	357,346	1,332,215
1936	720,200	291,920	1,012,120	1,072,663	395,983	1,468,646
1937	729,199	304,144	1,033,343	1,051,333	366,260	1,417,593
1938	755,744	307,225	1,062,969	1,027,369	366,457	1,393,826
1939	740,875	297,535	1,038,410	1,009,882	355,330	1,365,212
1940	617,187	141,864	759,051	716,018	370,136	1,086,154
1941	502,534	77,812	580,346	564,559	321,565	886,124
1942	400,418	56,829	457,247	501,000	344,763	845,763
1943	462,281	45,555	507,836	444,299	393,523	837,822
1944	473,918	63,425	537,343	508,270	365,825	874,095
1945	424,034	71,195	495,229	474,099	321,162	795,261
1946	485,462	83,227	568,689	647,795	291,046	938,841
1947	497,158	154,925	652,083	781,848	297,823	1,079,671
1948	526,574	213,244	739,818	924,359	332,530	1,256,889
1949	547,897	189,853	737,750	910,183	343,977	1,254,160
1950	622,963	213,879	863,842	910,379	319,585	1,229,964
1951	689,940	205,242	895,182	1,031,859	363,682	1,395,541
1952	710,205	178,438	888,643	1,025,420	362,668	1,388,088
1953	697,053	235,319	932,372	1,015,094	373,604	1,388,698
1954	706,743	292,119	998,862	1,046,356	357,259	1,403,615
1955	722,342	275,845	998,187	1,074,085	362,872	1,436,957
1956	727,165	286,791	1,013,956	1,052,157	357,026	1,409,183
1957	715,613	257,283	972,896	1,014,684	346,418	1,361,102
1958	713,168	279,685	992,853	1,095,698	321,379	1,417,077
1959	736,717	315,904	1,052,621	1,154,523	323,473	1,477,996

*Includes Goods exempt from Outward Rates from 1 October 1933
†Excludes Admiralty Vessels covered by Special Agreement for Appropriated berths for years from 1 October 1939 to 30 September 1946.

STATEMENT showing the Number of Arrivals of White Fishing Vessels and their Register Tonnage and the Quantity of Fish landed in each year from 1 October 1900

Year ending 30 September	Trawl fishing Vessels	Steam & Motor Line Vessels	Sail & Motor Yawls	†Tonnage of Vessels	Fish Landed
				Tons	Cwts.
1901	8,044	1,762	8,155	—	1,091,660
1902	9,197	1,843	6,062	—	1,217,680
1903	9,410	1,786	5,081	—	1,319,600
1904	9,125	1,825	5,675	—	1,463,640
1905	9,449	1,879	6,464	—	1,620,900
1906	9,136	1,708	6,554	—	1,485,700
1907	9,643	1,859	4,732	—	1,754,080
1908	10,712	2,170	3,863	—	1,994,020
1909	11,067	1,707	3,597	—	1,919,200
1910	11,596	1,555	2,729	—	2,000,800
1911	12,031	1,781	2,777	—	2,154,740
1912	11,275	1,668	1,952	826,300	2,256,960
1913	12,717	1,245	1,612	898,789	2,355,060
1914	12,082	1,436	1,111	858,544	2,268,860
1915	8,279	752	3,336	555,504	945,650
1916	6,487	677	3,826	414,236	672,111
1917	5,353	108	3,439	259,235	391,641
1918	3,759	495	5,575	207,818	304,378
1919	4,301	1,329	3,352	341,552	1,043,773
1920	8,852	1,242	3,030	676,781	1,764,988
1921	9,694	1,778	3,538	751,004	1,666,210
1922	10,403	2,383	3,288	842,045	2,086,652
1923	9,121	2,155	3,382	760,996	1,798,027
1924	12,298	1,781	1,810	1,008,308	2,523,141
1925	13,137	1,609	2,139	1,124,962	2,598,331
1926	12,918	1,208	2,030	1,076,888	2,446,679
1927	13,319	1,337	2,815	1,136,642	2,351,360
1928	14,458	1,324	2,487	1,223,866	2,216,748
1929	14,631	1,381	1,993	1,254,032	2,224,006
1930	15,762	1,207	2,135	1,344,565	2,274,532
1931	15,400	1,414	2,326	1,349,845	2,292,947
1932	16,024	1,448	1,811	1,392,486	2,167,648
1933	17,156	1,148	2,370	1,477,048	2,047,082
1934	17,177	1,408	2,832	1,502,210	1,905,048
1935	18,910	1,012	2,789	1,644,179	1,885,380
1936	17,218	901	2,336	1,526,134	1,764,368
1937	16,591	807	3,082	1,490,954	1,606,495
1938	16,054	892	3,110	1,460,472	1,783,435
1939	15,135	657	2,669	1,363,394	1,802,523
1940	9,443	340	2,589	832,058	1,347,334
1941	4,735	140	2,217	374,209	1,417,955
1942	4,121	47	1,875	285,301	1,338,202
1943	4,427	52	1,843	294,698	1,334,391
1944	3,894	,105	1,326	269,952	1,531,559
1945	4,358	144	1,563	306,079	1,742,624
1946	5,820	251	2,340	419,245	2,213,356

STATEMENT showing the Number of Arrivals of White Fishing Vessels and their Register Tonnage and the Quantity of Fish landed in each year from 1 October, 1900 (Continued)

Year ending 30 September	Trawl fishing Vessels	Steam & Motor Line Vessels	Sail & Motor Yawls	†Tonnage of Vessels	Fish Landed
1947	6,230	335	3,248	526,257	2,029,178
1948	6,435	409	2,683	583,187	2,066,306
1949	5,808	446	1,603	538,321	1,952,678
1950	7,846	620	1,488	642,788	1,744,005
1951	10,553	686	1,625	842,431	1,920,920
1952	12,311	505	802	973,869	1,855,216
1953	12,564	477	531	993,835	1,690,737
1954	11,172	485	728	924,108	1,689,231
1955	11,244	366	904	910,777	1,575,016
1956	11,918	365	719	936,212	1,735,276
1957	11,750	408	860	912,361	1,878,079
1958	11,652	446	619	893,202	1,921,488
1959	10,890	436	672	817,182	1,988,228

†No records available prior to 1912

STATISTICS

STATEMENT OF TRADE 1959–60 to 1972

Number of Vessels

Year	Coastwise	North Sea Oil	Foreign	New Vessels	White Fishing	Herring Fishing	Laid Up	Total
1959–60	1,847	—	611	22	11,437	911	420	15,248
1960–61	1,786	—	559	20	11,815	582	241	15,003
1961–62	1,768	—	504	11	12,409*	559	272	15,523
1962–63	1,706	—	513	9	11,416	746	239	14,629
1963–64	1,723	—	610	9	10,632	572	325	13,871
1964–65	1,812	—	633	14	10,410	597	304	13,770
1965–66	1,702	—	656	7	9,429	175	281	12,250
1966–67	1,689	—	751	6	9,410	77	328	12,261
1967–68	1,774	—	660	9	10,086	46	330	12,905
1968–69	2,213	—	827	10	10,557	137	791	14,535
1970	1,963	—	638	8	8,250	151	539	11,549
1971	2,366	—	656	9	6,074	28	407	9,540
1972	1,362	1,233	597	12	6,223	—	112	9,539

*Note the number of arrivals of White Fishing Vessels in 1961–62 included 1,717 arrivals of vessels engaged in drift net fishing for salmon.

a) North Sea Oil statistics were kept separately only from 1 January 1972

b) 1968–9 represents a period of 15 months due to the change of the Board's financial year end.

STATEMENT OF TRADE 1973 to 1985

Number of Vessels

Year	Coastwise	North Sea Oil	Foreign	New Vessels	White Fishing	Herring Fishing	Cruise Vessels	Total
1973	1,579	1,720	539	9	7,734	25	—	11,928
1974	1,341	2,865	361	3	7,158	67	—	12,025
1975	1,361	3,885	274	6	6,565	88	—	12,475
1976	1,355	3,895	277	7	5,903	102	—	13,090
1977	1,210	4,189	227	3	5,126	24	—	11,141
1978	1,078	4,046	172	5	5,148	46	—	10,810
1979	1,193	3,628	209	4	4,719	34	—	9,859
1980	1,096	3,719	165	3	4,813	10	—	9,806
1981	1,028	4,006	129	2	4,535	27	9	9,727
1982	1,030	3,932	72	2	4,616	—	5	9,652
1983	991	4,449	98	1	5,321	—	4	10,864
1984	1,035	4,854	77	3	4,955	20	4	10,948
1985	972	5,333	112	1	4,686	81	5	11,190

STATISTICS

STATEMENT OF TRADE 1959–60 to 1972

Net Register Tonnage of Vessels

Year	Coastwise	North Sea Oil	Foreign	New Vessels	White Fishing	Herring Fishing	Laid Up	Total
1959–60	739,215	—	340,137	10,168	714,427	47,328	60,624	1,911,899
1960–61	781,745	—	336,068	4,091	683,808	28,005	23,431	1,857,148
1961–62	814,677	—	324,821	4,599	689,587	27,701	30,007	1,891,392
1962–63	777,381	—	338,298	3,161	673,420	37,455	25,322	1,855,037
1963–64	745,853	—	368,565	4,944	659,408	28,792	39,439	1,847,001
1964–65	799,888	—	367,764	2,979	672,588	24,867	24,854	1,892,940
1965–66	738,396	—	364,017	3,675	657,934	9,701	32,292	1,806,015
1966–67	739,461	—	370,981	6,043	615,636	5,073	40,964	1,778,158
1967–68	780,411	—	328,614	5,760	650,138	3,338	32,262	1,800,523
1968–69	995,618	—	409,567	6,151	694,070	7,583	56,639	2,169,628
1970	804,271	—	278,598	3,145	546,456	7,974	47,521	1,687,965
1971	788,376	—	303,250	5,511	451,841	1,637	45,419	1,596,034
1972(1)	304,831	118,140	144,305	3,640	206,433	—	22,007	799,356
1972(2)	659,431	374,791	185,154	2,838	592,735	—	—	1,814,949

a) In period (2) of 1972 et sequin, the tonnages are stated gross, all other tonnages being stated net.
b) North Sea Oil statistics were kept separately only from 1 January 1972
c) 1968–9 represents a period of 15 months due to the change of the Board's financial year end.

STATISTICS

STATEMENT OF TRADE 1973 to 1985

Tonnage of Vessels

Year	Coastwise	North Sea Oil	Foreign	New Vessels	White Fishing	Herring Fishing	Cruise Vessels	Total
1973	1,318,432	1,076,783	437,488	2,520	1,320,858	1,294	—	4,232,631
1974	1,340,611	1,922,511	303,185	1,159	1,190,016	3,882	—	4,837,462
1975	1,364,289	2,755,622	214,202	6,004	1,011,003	5,892	—	5,454,517
1976	1,371,519	2,868,050	241,698	6,246	897,682	5,270	—	5,911,642
1977	1,487,175	3,284,867	324,373	2,652	708,505	1,000	—	5,867,982
1978	1,208,115	3,624,160	269,517	2,105	676,217	1,646	—	5,830,149
1979	1,703,819	3,212,579	253,949	2,376	554,966	1,826	—	5,729,515
1980	1,680,010	3,487,840	231,464	1,677	434,398	1,980	—	5,837,369
1981	1,595,405	3,778,723	164,728	1,417	378,185	1,279	42,254	5,919,737
1982	1,609,982	3,605,403	103,578	3,747	326,083	—	27,793	5,648,793
1983	1,584,080	4,384,984	95,797	763	382,160	—	18,575	6,466,359
1984	1,584,946	4,931,956	104,298	2,289	329,591	7,155	15,581	6,939,816
1985	1,553,750	5,649,838	123,661	763	308,236	12,283	21,832	7,670,363

STATEMENT OF TRADE 1959–60 to 1972

Year	Tonnage of Goods Imported			Tonnage of Goods Exported			Total Tonnage of Goods Imported and Exported
	Coastwise	Foreign	Total	Coastwise	Foreign	Total	
1959–60	767,897	339,930	1,107,827	211,761	47,737	259,498	1,367,325
1960–61	778,415	313,445	1,091,860	155,507	21,256	176,763	1,268,623
1961–62	791,295	308,225	1,099,520	147,030	27,870	174,900	1,274,420
1962–63	772,343	357,198	1,129,541	151,028	25,186	176,214	1,305,755
1963–64	770,475	414,760	1,185,235	136,310	28,358	164,668	1,349,903
1964–65	812,715	382,585	1,195,336	140,245	62,942	203,187	1,398,523
1965–66	803,704	365,009	1,168,713	120,255	75,124	195,379	1,364,092
1966–67	812,498	389,619	1,202,117	112,519	80,894	193,413	1,395,530
1967–68	870,326	389,277	1,259,603	116,640	62,353	178,993	1,438,596
1968–69	1,044,119	538,438	1,582,557	146,903	73,064	219,967	1,802,524
1970	908,185	378,005	1,286,190	126,808	64,199	191,007	1,477,197
1971	864,776	405,348	1,270,124	174,859	44,381	219,240	1,489,364
1972	897,497	374,352	1,271,849	225,321	51,071	276,392	1,548,241

STATEMENT OF TRADE 1973 to 1985

Year	Tonnage of Goods Imported			Tonnage of Goods Exported			Total Tonnage of Goods Imported and Exported
	Coastwise	Foreign	Total	Coastwise	Foreign	Total	
1973	978,871	381,689	1,360,560	304,676	41,511	346,187	1,706,747
1974	1,015,045	385,020	1,400,065	404,881	28,277	433,158	1,833,223
1975	1,008,207	276,147	1,284,354	472,291	33,087	505,378	1,789,732
1976	1,019,407	289,641	1,309,048	562,825	22,610	585,435	1,894,483
1977	799,413	269,574	1,068,987	642,056	15,330	657,386	1,726,373
1978	752,069	266,493	1,018,562	732,194	31,900	764,094	1,782,656
1979	1,038,000	285,000	1,323,000	878,000	49,000	927,000	2,250,000
1980	1,085,000	217,000	1,302,000	936,000	23,000	959,000	2,261,000
1981	1,031,367	187,616	1,218,983	1,044,753	34,577	1,080,330	2,299,313
1982	1,023,000	189,092	1,212,092	963,851	40,822	1,004,673	2,216,765
1983	1,214,691	215,810	1,430,501	1,032,874	56,147	1,089,021	2,519,522
1984	1,196,270	263,014	1,459,284	1,144,071	47,390	1,191,461	2,650,745
1985	1,286,844	171,490	1,458,334	1,274,643	49,803	1,324,446	2,782,780

Appendix 4

PERSONAE DRAMATIS

Some of the many office bearers directly concerned in the operation and development of Aberdeen Harbour down the centuries. The list is necessarily incomplete. Many of the names are no longer known, and a great many have been excluded due to space limitations.

CHAIRMEN—HARBOUR COMMISSIONERS AND EARLIER
From earliest times the Chief Magistrate, and later the Lord Provost, was the chairman of the governing body. With the formation of the Aberdeen Harbour Commissioners, the Lord Provost continued as Chairman until 1960.

CHAIRMEN—ABERDEEN HARBOUR BOARD

1960–66	Richard Irvin CBE
1966–78	Roger J C Fleming OBE, TD, DL, JP
1978–84	George M Lawrence MA, LL B, TD
1984–	John W Cradock CA

HARBOUR MANAGER

1937–47	James Hay Petrie OBE

GENERAL MANAGERS

1947–57	James Hay Petrie OBE
1957–78	Norman R Beattie JP CA
1978–	Captain John R Turner MCIT, MIMH, MNI

HARBOUR CLERKS
The duties of Harbour Clerk were generally performed on a part time basis by the Town Clerk of the City of Aberdeen up to 1960. After reconstitution in 1961 the post of Secretary was created and combined with the title of General Manager until 1978 from whence until 1979, the title was combined with that of Deputy General Manager.

1793–c1838	William Carnegie
c1838–75	John Angus
1887–1924	William Gordon
1924–26	James W Davidson
1926–42	George S Fraser MA, BL
1943–46	D G Bunn
1946–60	J C Rennie

219

SECRETARY

1978–79	James Will CA
1979–	James R Scott ACCA

COLLECTORS

One of the earliest recorded titles for a Harbour Official—forerunner of modern Harbour Treasurers. The post was appointed annually.

1596–7	Alexander Kempt		1637–38	Adame Gordone
1597–8	James Menzies		1638–39	Alexander Ramsey
1598–9	Alexander Burnet		1639–43	Patrick Moir
1599–1600	James Menzies		1943–44	Hendrie Dun
1605–06	Alexander Kempe		1644–45	Alexander Ramsey
1608–09	Walter Menzies Jr		1645–7	Gilbert Mollesone
1609–10	Thomas Johnstoune		1647–	Charles Robertson
1610–11	William Gordon		1647–48	Androw Raitt
1611–12	Alexander Cruickshank		1648–49	John Galloway
1612–13	Alexander Rowen		1649–50	Alexander Watson
1613–14	Thomas Tullidaff		1650–51	Alexander Burnet
1614–15	Alexander Kempe		1651–52	Johne Ray
1615–16	William Forbes Jr		1652–55	John Scott Sr
1618	George Andersone		1655–56	Androw Burnet
1618–21	Thomas Gray		1656–57	Thomas Merser
1621–22	Thomas Cargill		1657–58	James Ewine
1622–23	Thomas Gray		1658–59	James Brown
1623–24	Robert Cruickshank		1659–60	Normand Leslie
1624–25	George Morrissoun		1660–61	Johne Gordone
1625–26	Androw Meldrum		1661–62	Gilbert Black
1626–27	Robert Cruickshank		1662–63	Patrick Logan
1628–29	Robert Smythe		1663–65	Alexander Burnet
1629–30	Jhon Lesly		1665–66	Alexander Gordoun
1630–31	Charles Kelle		1666–67	Robert Cruickshank
1631–34	James Robertson		1667–68	William Bissit
1634–35	Paull Menzies		1668–69	George Burnet
1636–37	John Alexander		1669–70	Alexander Walker

HARBOUR TREASURER AND COLLECTOR

1810–17	Alexander Young
1817–42	James Riddell
1842–79	Alexander Reid
1879–92	Peter Riddel
1892–1925	James Ross
1926–57	J Hay Petrie OBE
1957–60	Norman R Beattie CA, JP
1960–78	James Will CA
1978–	David I Holmes CA

HARBOUR OVERSEER

c1751	Arthur Gibbon

HARBOUR ENGINEERS

1809–16	John Gibb
1829–33	John Gibb
1840–67	James Abernethy CE
1867–80	William Dyce Cay CE
1880–95	William Smith CE
1895–1931	R Gordon Nicol MInstCE
1931–42	Hugh R Barr AMInstCE
1942–60	John Anderson MICE, MIStruct E, MInstT
1960–68	Andrew Aitken, MICE, MIMechE
1968–75	Malcolm H Chapman, BSc, MICE, MASCE
1976–	R Barclay Braithwaite BSc, CEng, MICE, MASCE

HARBOUR MASTER

1821– ?	Captain James Mitchell
? –1857	Captain Alexander Morrison
1857–67	Captain James Gauld
1867–89	Captain William Clark
1889–1922	Captain W Allen Crombie
1922–39	Captain Thomas A Wyness
1939–48	Captain W G Johnstone
1948–50	Captain John W Coultas
1950–53	Captain Ian P Posgate
1953–67	Captain Lindsay Traill
1967–69	Captain George Hay
1969–	Captain Brian Atkinson MNI

Bibliography

Aberdeen Almanac

Aberdeen City Council (1890) Charters relating to the Burgh of Aberdeen

Aberdeen Directory

Aberdeen Harbour Accounts 1891–1985

Aberdeen Harbour Handbooks (1933–1985)

Allan, R C *The Landing of the Queen at Aberdeen 8th September 1848* (Taylor & Henderson 1848)

Clark, Victoria E *The Port of Aberdeen* (D Wyllie & Son 1921)

Duthie, Dr J L *To the Rescue! Life-saving at Aberdeen 1802–1924* (Rainbow Books 1981)

'History of a Great Industry—21 years of Steam Trawling' *People's Journal*, (Aberden 1903)

Gordon, George, The Shore Porters Society of Aberdeen 1498–1968

Gray, Tide Tables 1844–73

Keith, Alexander *A Thousand Years of Aberdeen* (Aberdeen University Press 1972)

McKenzie, W Third Statistical Account of Scotland, City of Aberdeen (Oliver & Boyd 1953)

Minutes and Reports of the Aberdeen Harbour Commissioners

Minutes and Reports of the Aberdeen Harbour Board

Parliamentary Evidence, Aberdeen Harbour Bill 1810 (Harbour Trustees)

Parliamentary Evidence, Aberdeen Harbour Bill 1828 (Harbour Trustees)

Parliamentary Evidence, Aberdeen Harbour Bill 1839 (Harbour Trustees)

Port Labour in Aberdeen and Glasgow: Report of the Board of Inquiry 1937 (HMSO)

Record of Events in Aberdeen and the North 1801–1927 (Aberdeen Newspapers Limited 1928)

Registrum Episcopatus Aberdonensis (Spalding Club 1845)

Rochdale, Lord Report of the Court of Inquiry into the Major Ports of Great Britain (HMSO 1962)

Shipping Lists 1822–42

Somerville, Robert *Scotia Pontifica* (Clarendon Press, Oxford 1982)

Souvenir Brochure of Aberdeen Fish Market (Aberdeen City Council, 1939)

Statistical Account of Scotland 1791–99

Taylor, Louise B *Aberdeen Shore Work Accounts 1596–1670* (Aberdeen University Press 1972

Wilson, David F *Dockers* (Fontana/Collins 1972)

Wyness, Fenton *City by the Grey North Sea* (Impulse Books 1972)

Index